ACE YOUR NEXT JOB INTERVIEW IN EMBEDDED SYSTEMS AND IOT SOFTWARE

250+ behavioral, technical questions & answers

Akram Mohammad

ACE YOUR NEXT JOB INTERVIEW IN EMBEDDED SYSTEMS AND IOT SOFTWARE, FIRST EDITION

Published by Outcomes Foundry LLC, Austin, TX

For more information, contact OutcomesFoundry@gmail.com

Introduction

Embedded Systems continues to change the world and the recent explosion of "Internet of Things" is connecting people to devices at home and work. Despite its many applications, the basics of Embedded Systems remain the same, and a deep understanding of its concepts, architecture, and programming will enable the candidate to succeed in any job interview and perform well on the job long after receiving the offer.

This book translates many years of interviewing experience into written form.

Who this book is for and not?

The book is for you if

- You are already familiar with Embedded systems/IoT concepts, design, operating systems and programming and want to deepen your understanding of them.
- You want to revise topics you already know.
- You want to learn how to approach a problem.
- You want to learn to use a whiteboard in an artificial environment.
- You want to learn how to articulate what you know to the interviewer in a way that will impress him/her.
- Secure the job that you will love and continue loving it.

This books NOT for you if

- This is your first embedded system, operating system, IoT or programming book.
- You do not want to get up and use a whiteboard in an interview.
- You do not love problem-solving.
- You do not want to practice the answers to the questions.

What's inside

Embedded systems/RTOS

6. What is an Embedded System vs. Real-time system vs. RTOS

7. What are hard and soft real-time systems?

8. Explain little-endian vs. big-endian?

9. How to decide if a processor is using little-endian format or big-endian format?

Interrupts

10. What is an Interrupt handler?

11. What is Interrupt latency?

12. What stack does the Interrupt handler use?

13. What are some common issues when handling Interrupts?

14. How do you measure Interrupt latency?

15. What is a nested Interrupt?

16. What are conforming and non-conforming Interrupt routines?

17. What are their advantages and disadvantages?

Processes

18. What is a process vs. thread?

Critical sections

19. What is a Critical section?

20. What is race condition?

21. What is MUTEX?

22. What is the difference between MUTEX and semaphore?

23. What is a spinlock?

24. What is a deadlock and how can you resolve it?

25. What is priority Inversion?

26. How does the priority inheritance protocol work?

27. For each of the following situations, discuss which shared-data protection mechanisms seem most likely and why?

Scheduler

28. What type of scheduling is there in RTOS or Embedded OS?

29. What are the typical states of a task in an embedded OS?

30. Consider this statement:

Timers

31. What is a watchdog timer?

32. What are the various uses of timers in an embedded system?

Memory

33. How does the program memory areas in an embedded operating system?

34. Reasonable design of memory management

Embedded programming

35. What makes the code Re-entrant?

36. What do you protect shared data?

37. How does the debugger work?

38. What is the difference between a hardware breakpoint vs. a software breakpoint?

39. What is the need for an infinite loop in embedded systems?

40. What is the stack overflow?

41. What is the cause of the stack overflow?

42. What are the start-up code steps?

43. How to access the fixed memory location in embedded C?

44. What are the common causes of a segmentation fault in C?

45. What is the difference between Segmentation fault and Bus error?

46. Consider a system that controls the traffic lights as a major intersection.

Embedded hardware

47. What are the mechanisms used to configure modern Systems-on-chips at reset?

48. How many wires are required to reliably implement TTL-like serial communication between two devices, and why?

49. Why are 8-bit microcontrollers still used when 32-bit & 64-bit microcontrollers exist?

50. Mention what buses are used for communication in an embedded system?

51. What is the difference between a microprocessor and a micro-controller?

52. What is a DMA and how does the DMA work?

53. What is the difference between a driver and firmware?

54. Does DMA deal with physical or virtual address?

55. What are the main functions of a multiplexed address and a data bus?

56. What are the different types of buses used by embedded systems?

57. Why the vast majority of high performance embedded systems use RISC & why**?**

58. What is a Raspberry Pi?

59. What are GPIO Pins?

60. What is a Thermocouple, and how does it work?

61. What is PWM (Pulse Width Modulation)?

62. What is the difference between the I2c and SPI communication Protocols?

63. What is the difference between Asynchronous and Synchronous Communication?

64. What is the difference between RS232 and RS485?

65. What is the difference between Bit Rate and Baud Rate?

66. What is the difference between Asynchronous and Synchronous Communication?

67. What is I2C (Inter-Integrated Circuit) communication?

68. What is a bus arbitration?

69. What is CAN bus?

70. What is CSMA/CA and CSMA/CD in CAN Communication?

71. What is bit stuffing?

72. What does the timing diagram of a static RAM look like?

73. Design a circuit?

74. What are the (dis) advantages of edge-triggered & level-triggered Interrupts?

75. Why is FIFO useful for received bytes in a UART?

76. How might you driver an LED if your microprocessor does not have any I/O pins?

Experience-based

77. What debugging tools did you use?

78. What type of source control software did you use?

79. If a system crashes, what can do to figure out what happened?

80. What does a map file contain?

81. When memory is a constraint, is it preferable to allocate memory statically or dynamically?

82. What are the pro and cons of using a generic RTOS on a mid-range microcontroller?

83. What are the characteristics of UART/RS-232, I2C, and SPI communication?

84. What are C and C++ still widely supported in embedded firmware development?

85. Are firmware and data embedded in microcontrollers generally safe from downloading, tampering, or hacking?

86. What are some of the commonly found errors in embedded systems?

87. Which one is better? Down_to_zero loop or Count_up_loops?

88. How to reduce function call overhead in ARM-based systems?

89. What are the considerations when buying an embedded operating system?

Technical questions (Coding)

C programming

General

90.   Define the following: union, static, const, volatile, void *, extern, %, &, enum

91.   What does the keyword const mean?

92.   When should the register modifier be used? Does it really help?

93.   What do the following declarations mean?

94.   How is a "union" different from a "struct" in "C"?

95.   What is the difference between (A && B) and (A & B) ?

96.   What is the advantage of a macro over a function?

97.   What is the difference between int (* comp)(char *, char *) and int *comp (char *, char *)?

98.   What happens on the call stack when a subroutine is called?

99.   What is the size of int?

100.   What are the typical sizes of int, char and float data type?

101.   What is a void pointer in C?

102.   In a function when do we use heap memory vs. stack memory?

103.   What happens when you overload the stack?

104. Which data structure is used to perform recursion?

105. How do you multiply a variable by 8 without using the multiplication operator?

106. How can you check to see whether a symbol is defined?

107. How do you override a define macro?

108. How do you print an address?

109. How can you send an unlimited number of arguments to a function?

110. What is the benefit of using an enum rather than a #define const?

111. What is the difference between a string copy(strcpy) and a memory copy (memcpy)?

112. What is loop unrolling?

113. What is the memory leak in C?

114. What are dangling pointers?

115. What is the difference between pass-by-value and pass-by-reference in c?

116. Can do I define a structure without holes in it?

117. Is this function reentrant?

118. Is this function reentrant?

Find the output

119.   What is the value of a at the end of each line?

120.   What is the value of a, b and c at the end of each line?

121.   What is the value of z at the end of main()?

122.   What does the following code do?

123.   What does the following code fragment output and why?

124.   Which method if any, is preferred and why?

Identify errors

125.   What is the difference between const *myPtr and char *const myPtr?

126.   Why does the assert fail?

127.   What is wrong with this code?

128.   What is wrong with this code?

129.   What is wrong with this code?

130.   What is wrong with this code?

131.   What is the problem with the below code?

132.   What is wrong with the following code fragment?

133.   What is wrong with this Interrupt routine ?

134.   Where to use semaphores in the following code to make the function reentrant?

Bit manipulation

135. Write a code snippet to swap endian?

136. Embedded systems always require the user to manipulate bits in registers or variables.

137. Set an integer variable at the absolute address 0x6789 to the value 0xaabb?

138. Count set bits in a number.

139. How to toggle a particular bit in C?

140. Write the macros to set, clear, toggle, and check the bit of a given integer?

141. Write MACRO to swap the bytes in 32bit Integer Variable?

Write code

142. Write the MIN macro that is, a macro that takes two arguments and returns the smaller of the two arguments?

143. How do you create an infinite loop in embedded C?

144. Using the variable a, give the definitions for the following:

145. Write your own string copy function?

146. Write your own memory copy function?

147. Write your own swap function which exchanges the values of two integers and the swap caller?

148. Write a function to take a pointer to a singly linked list

149. Write your own integer to string conversion program?

150. Reverse a singly linked list?

151. Delete a node in double linked list?

152. Reverse a string

153. Write a function to Insert a node a sorted linked list?

154. Write a function to Convert a string to upper case?

155. Write a function to find the factorial of a number?

156. Write a function to get Fibonacci number?

157. Write a function that finds the last instance of a character in a string?

C++ programming

General

158. What is a friend function? Can we access the private member of the friend?

159. What is a copy constructor?

160. When are copy constructors called in C++?

161. Why copy constructor takes the parameter as a reference in C++?

162. Why copy constructor argument should be const in C++?

163. What is the difference between copy constructor & assignment operator?

164. What is destructor in C++? When is the destructor called?

165. Distinguish between shallow copy and deep copy?

166. Is it possible to overload the destructor of the class?

167. What do you mean by pure virtual function?

168. What is a virtual function? Why are there no virtual constructors but there are virtual destructors in C++?

169. Can we have a virtual destructor in C++? When to use virtual destructors?

170. What is "this" pointer?

171. What is a namespace?

172. What is function overloading in C++?

173. What is Overriding?

174. How do you call a C module within a C++ module?

175. What is name mangling? And why do C++ compilers need it?

176. What is a dangling pointer?

177. What is a memory leak?

178. What is inline function?

179. What are the differences between a struct in C and C++?

180. What is The Order of Calling for The Constructors and Destructors in Case of Objects of Inherited Classes?

181.   Explain the order of constructor and destructor calls in case of multiple inheritance?

182.   What is name mangling? Provide an example?

183.   Why is the size of an empty class not zero in C++?

184.   What is the difference between a C++ struct and C++ class?

185.   What is encapsulation?

186.   What Is Inheritance?

Bit manipulation

187.   Write a function to display an integer in a binary format?

Advanced topics

Compilers & loaders

188.   What is a compiler?

189.   What is a loader?

190.   What is a linker?

191.   Define a Symbol Table?

192.   What is a cross compiler?

193.   Give examples for : compile-time error, link-time error and run time error?

194.   What is the difference between static linking and dynamic linking?

195. How does the compilation/linking process work?

Networking

196. What is IP, TCP, UDP?

197. What is a socket?

198. Compare between TCP/IP & OSI model?

199. Is UDP better than TCP? Can you list the UDP and TCP packet formats?

200. What is the TCP 3-way handshake?

201. What does a socket consist of?

202. What is socket programming?

Embedded Linux

203. What is embedded Linux? Provide examples?

204. What is the difference between Linux and Embedded Linux?

205. Which Linux OS is best for embedded development?

206. Why Linux is used in an embedded system?

207. What are the elements of embedded Linux?

208. Can we use semaphore or mutex or spinlock in the Interrupt context in Linux kernel?

vxWorks

209. What is vxWorks?

210.   What are the benefits of vxWorks and why?

211.   What is the memory layout in vxWorks?

212.   What is the difference between signals and Interrupts?

213.   What are message queues and Pipes in vxWorks?

214.   What Is the Difference B/w downloadable and Bootable Application?

215.   What is Tornado and its features?

216.   What does the target server do?

217.   What is task spawn in vxWorks?

218.   What are message queues and pipes?

219.   How is vxWorks different from UNIX or Linux OS?

220.   What are the differences between traditional UNIX and vxWorks?

221.   What kind of products has been developed using vxWorks?

222.   How does vxWorks system calls work?

223.   Why can't I call printf() inside Interrupt service routines?

224.   Is there a better malloc/free replacement that does not fragment as badly?

225.   Is there a better malloc/free replacement that does not fragment as badly?

226. What is saving and restoring floating point registers per context switch and in an ISR?

227. What are vxWorks "watchdog" related common errors?

228. What are the common parameters to tune for better network performance on vxWorks?

229. Can I get multiple target shell sessions via telnet?

Internet of Things (IoT)

230. What is IoT and how does it work?

231. Describe the different components of IoT?

232. What is the use of BLE in IoT?

233. What are the benefits and challenges of IoT?

234. Name some of the various sectors where IoT played a major role?

235. What are the security concerns related to IoT?

236. Explain the IoT protocol stack?

237. What is the top 5 Machine to Machine (M2M) applications?

238. What Is The difference between IoT and Machine to Machine (m2m)?

239. What is Industrial Internet of Things (IIoT)?

240. What are the main challenges of implementing IoT?

241. What are the industrial applications for wireless sensor networks Internet of Things (IoT)?

242. What is the difference between IoT devices and embedded devices?

243. What are the most used sensors types in IoT?

244. Can you list out some of water sensors?

245. What is data collection in IoT?

246. What is IoT cloud?

247. What role does network play in the IoT?

248. What is the difference between IoT devices and embedded devices?

249. What is sharding?

250. What is the difference b/w a wireless sensor network (WSN) and the IoT network?

251. Why is Zigbee protocol so important for the Internet of Things implementation?

252. Explain Bluetooth Low Energy (BLE) Protocol for Internet of Things (IoT)?

253. What are the most commonly used protocols in IoT?

254. What is meant by a smart city in the context of IoT?

255. What sensor and actuator are used to control any home appliances from any IoT devices in wired mode?

256. What are suitable databases for Iot?

257. What are the enabling factors of IoT?

258. What is an IoT platform?

259. What is edge computing?

260. What is Condition-based maintenance?

261. What is predictive maintenance?

262. What impact will IoT have on the Manufacturing sector?

263. What is IoT ThingWorx?

264. Explain IoT GE Predix?

265. What is Big Data and How it is related to IoT?

Azure IoT

266. What is Azure IoT?

267. What is Windows 10 IoT Core?

268. What is Azure RTOS?

269. What is Azure IoT Edge?

270. What is Azure IoT Hub?

271. What are the azure technologies/services available for creating IoT solutions?

AWS IoT

272. How does AWS IoT?

Strategies to answer Interview questions

Before Interview

- **Create Worksheets** – Write personalized answers to key questions using a framework like STAR (Situation, Task, Action, Result)
- **Learn to draw** architecture diagrams – Practice drawing every story, concept, and solution.
- **Find practice partners** - Practicing with others will give a fresh perspective, moral support and keeps you accountable

During the Interview

- **Use whiteboard** – Effective whiteboard usage increases your success rate exponentially, especially for technical rounds. Start by writing the problem statement on the whiteboard, ask clarification questions, list assumptions & requirements. Draw and write your answers as points on a whiteboard.
- **Structure, Structure & Structure** – Use a framework to structure your answer for clarity

After the interview

- **Connect with the interviewer** – by sending a thank you letter and a connection request via LinkedIn.

For technical questions

- **Practice writing code** on paper before trying it on a computer
- **Answering framework**
    - Listen to the question and clarify as needed
    - Try with an example and test edge conditions
    - Optimize the code and say it out loud as you do
    - Write the code in the language you are most comfortable in
    - Test code with the interviewer
    - Be smart but not smarter (then the interviewer)

Behavioral questions

1. Elevator script

Best practice

- Keep the pitch to < 2 minutes
- Wire script as points and rehearse it until you can say it in sleep
- The script should include 3 major skills for the role you seek

Framework/sample

- Hello, my name is ___
- I have about 20 years of experience in companies such as X, Y, Z
- My current role is the lead architect. I lead a team of 10 architects at company X
- As an Engineer, I have architected a major cloud migration project
- As a Lead, I have mentored 3 senior architects

2. Tell me about yourself?

Best Practice

- Pick 3-5 main requirements from the job description
- Highlight your last 3 jobs where you did similar work using the same verbiage in the job description
- End your story by highlighting "why you are looking for a job" and additionally "Why this company and or role"

Framework/Sample

- I'm currently <role A> for <company B>
- As part of this role I do <Work C> (using verbiage from the job description)
- I'd love to highlight <results D>
- Repeat 2-3 times
    - Before that, I was<role E> for <company F>
    - As part of this role, I did <work G>
    - I'd love to highlight <results H>
    - Additionally, I have <education I>
    - I'm leaving my current role because of <reason J>
    - And I'm excited about this opportunity with <your company> for the following reasons - <Reason 1>, <reason 2>, <Reason 3>

3. Why this role/company/industry?

Best practice

- Summarize the answer to the question then give 3 reasons
- Talk about the company
- Talk about the job/role/position
- Talk about the culture and values

Framework/Sample

- There are 3 specific reasons why the <role of a role A> or <I'd like to join company B> or < I'd love to join industry C> is appealing to me:
    - <reason why you like the role?
    - <reason why you like the company and its culture?
    - <reason why you like the industry?

4. What are your short-term or long-term goals?

Best practice

- Summarize your long-term goal
- Talk about your short-term goal - this job
- Talk about the company
- Talk about the values/culture

Framework/sample

- In the long run, I see myself becoming < next level position>, where I can do <next level responsibilities?
- To get there my short term goal is to find a position that <responsibilities of the current role?
- Additionally, I'd want to this at a company such as <Company's name> that encourages <culture/values>

5. Describe a situation when you … ?

Best practice

- Specify the dramatic situation you came into
- Talk about the goals that you intended to achieve and the metric and target to measure
- Talk about the actions you took in the situation
- Talk about the results that we achieved

Sample Questions?

- Leadership & influence
  - Tell me about a time when you had to make an unpopular decision?
  - Tell me about a time when you showed initiative?
- Challenges
  - Tell me about a time when you weren't able to reach a deadline?
  - How did you deal with a difficult boss?
- Successes/Failures
  - What do you think is your biggest success?
  - Tell me about a time when you solved a problem creatively?
- Teamwork
  - Tell me about a time when you had to do something you didn't want to do?
  - How would you deal with difficult co-workers?

Technical questions (Concepts)

Operating Systems

Embedded systems/RTOS

6. What is an Embedded System vs. Real-time system vs. RTOS

   Answer:

   An Embedded system is a system using the microprocessor to handle the processes and using the CPU chip to permanently store programs in ROM or flash memory.

   Embedded OS is an operating system that proves services to embedded hardware or systems. Examples are vxWorks, QNX, LynxOS, pSOS, Nucleus RTX, Linux, Win CE, Integrity, etc.

   A real-time system is a system that must respond to the events within a certain time. A real-time operating system is an operating system that can run real-time processes successfully

   The real-time operating system is an operating system designed for use in real-time systems. Examples are eCoS, RTLinux, LynxOS, QNX, etc.

7. What are hard and soft real-time systems?

   Answer:

The hard real-time systems are the ones that depend on the output very strictly on time. Any late response or delay cannot be tolerated and will always be considered a failure. The soft real-time systems on the other are not very rigid as the hard real-time systems. The performance of the system degrades with the lateness of response, but it is bearable and can be optimized to a certain level for reuse of the result.

8. Explain little-endian vs. big-endian?

Answer:

All computers do not store the bytes that comprise a multi-byte value in the same order. Consider a 16-bit internet that is made up of 2 bytes. Two ways to store this value –

Little Endian – In this scheme, low-order byte is stored on the starting address (A) and high-order byte is stored on the next address (A + 1).

Big Endian – In this scheme, high-order byte is stored on the starting address (A) and low-order byte is stored on the next address (A + 1).

Example: 0x12674592 in 32 bit representation can be stores as below

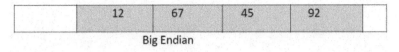

0x00400000 0x00400001 0x00400002 0x00400003

	12	67	45	92	

Big Endian

0x00400000 0x00400001 0x00400002 0x00400003

	92	45	67	12	

Little Endian

9. How to decide if a processor is using little-endian format or big-endian format?

Answer:

Write a small below program to find out if the process is little-endian or big-endian

```
void print_endian() {
        unsigned inti = 1;
        char *c = (char*) &I;

        If (*c) printf ("\n Little Endian")
        else
         printf ("\n Big Endian")
}
```

Interrupts

10. What is an Interrupt handler?

Answer:

An Interrupt is a signal that gets the attention of the CPU and is usually generated when I/O is required. When an Interrupt occurs, control is transferred to the operating system, which determines the action to be taken. Interrupts are prioritized; the higher the priority, the faster the Interrupt will be serviced.

The occurrence of an event is usually signaled by an Interrupt from either hardware or software. Hardware may trigger an Interrupt at any time by sending a signal to the CPU. The software may trigger an Interrupt by executing a system call. When the CPU is Interrupted, it stops what it is doing and immediately transfers execution to a fixed location containing the starting address where the service routine for the Interrupt is located. The Interrupt service routine will call the Interrupt-handler to proceed with the Interrupt. After the Interrupt is serviced, the CPU resumes the Interrupt computation.

Two Interrupt request lines:

- NMI(Non maskable Interrupt) which is used for events such as unrecoverable memory errors.
- MI(Maskable Interrupt) which is used by device controllers to request service.

11. What is Interrupt latency?

Answer:

Interrupt latency is the time that elapses from when an Interrupt is generated when the source of the Interrupt is serviced. For many operating systems, devices are serviced as soon as the device's Interrupt handler is executed. Interrupt latency may be affected by microprocessor design, Interrupt controllers, Interrupt masking, and the operating system's (OS) Interrupt handling methods.

12. What stack does the Interrupt handler use?

Answer:

It depends based on the Operating system configuration. In most scenarios, the kernel stack is used to handled Interrupt routines. However, the operating systems can be configured to use a specific stack for Interrupts.

13. What are some common issues when handling Interrupts?

Answer:

Interrupt handlers almost always need to finish their execution quickly—the details depend on the device and application—and this limits the complexity of what can be done in their code. Also, the context in which the Interrupt handler code is executed can, for either hardware or software reasons, prevent the user from within the Interrupt handler code of:

- Common library functions
- Access to peripherals and devices
- Even certain types of CPU instructions

The usual way to mitigate this is to have the Interrupt controller set a special variable that is observed by non-Interrupt code, and which can then perform arbitrary actions.

14. How do you measure Interrupt latency?

Answer:

With the help of the oscilloscope, we can measure the Interrupt latency. You need to take the following steps.

- The first takes two GPIOs.
- Configure one GPIO to generate the Interrupt and second for the toggling (if you want you can attach an LED).
- Monitor the PIN (using the oscilloscope or analyzer) which you have configured to generate the Interrupt.
- Also, monitor (using the oscilloscope or analyzer) the second pin which is toggled at the beginning of the Interrupt service routine.
- When you will generate the Interrupt then the signal of both GPIOs will change.

The interval between the two signals (Interrupt latency) may be easily read from the instrument.

15. What is a nested Interrupt?

Answer:

In a nested Interrupt system, an Interrupt is allowed to anytime and anywhere even an ISR is being executed. But, only the highest priority ISR will be executed immediately. The second highest priority ISR will be executed after the highest one is completed.

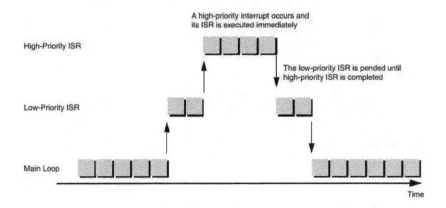

The rules of a nested Interrupt system are:

- All Interrupts must be prioritized.
- After initialization, any Interrupts are allowed to occur anytime and anywhere.

- If a low-priority ISR is Interrupted by a high-priority Interrupt, the high-priority ISR is executed.
- If a high-priority ISR is Interrupted by a low-priority Interrupt, the high-priority ISR continues executing.
- The same priority ISRs must be executed by time order

16. What are conforming and non-conforming Interrupt routines?

Answer:

Confirming routines tell the RTOS when they enter and exit and non-confirming routines do not.

17. What are their advantages and disadvantages?

Answer:

The primary advantage of a nonconforming Interrupt routine is that it can be faster since it avoids the overhead associated with letting the RTOS know when it enters and exits. The disadvantages are that the nonconforming Interrupt routines may not call any of the RTOS functions and that they must not allow themselves to be Interrupted by any higher-priority Interrupt routine that might call the RTOS.

Processes

18. What is a process vs. thread?

Answer:

The process is a program in execution and thread is a single sequence stream within a process

Similarities

- Like processes, threads share CPU and only one thread active (running) at a time.
- Like processes, threads within a process execute sequentially.
- Like processes, a thread can create children.
- And like process, if one thread is blocked, another thread can run.

Differences

- Unlike processes, threads are not independent of one another.
- Unlike processes, all threads can access every address in the task.
- Unlike processes, a thread is designed to assist one other. Note that processes might or might not assist one another because processes may originate from different users.

Critical sections

19. What is a Critical section?

Answer:

Critical Section is the part of the program where the shared memory is accessed. A non-re-entrant piece of code that can only be executed by one process or thread at a time. A set of statements that can have only one process executing it at a time is a critical section

20. What is race condition?

Answer:

Whenever two or more processes or threads are reading and writing the shared modifiable data at the same time, it is possible that one process or thread will interfere with the others, and this situation is called race condition.

Race conditions can be fixed by careful design of task priorities, mutual exclusions, critical sections, etc.

An example would be a race between a UI task and a background task that updates information for UI display. If the UI task is pre-empted while in the process of updating the UI screen and the background task updates the underlying displayed information, then the information presented to the end-user may be non-coherent.

21. What is MUTEX?

Answer:

Mutex is used to make sure that if one process is using shared modifiable data, the other processes will be excluded from doing the same thing. A mutex is an object that can be locked and unlocked.

Each critical section or access to shared data is protected by a mutex. To enter the critical section, or read/write the shared data:

- lock the mutex (this blocks until the mutex is free to lock)
- enter the critical section to read/write the shared data
- unlock the mutex.

When a process wants to enter its critical section, it first tests the lock. If the lock is 0, the process first sets it to 1 and then enters the critical section. If the lock is already 1, the process just waits until the (lock) variable becomes 0. Thus, a 0 means that no process in its critical section and 1 means hold your horses - some process is in its critical section. Mutex is a semaphore with values limited to 1 or 0.

22. What is the difference between MUTEX and semaphore?

Answer

- A mutex can be considered as a binary semaphore.

- A mutex is owned by the thread which locked it (that is, only the process which locked the mutex can unlock it). Whereas a semaphore can be changed by another thread or process.
- Semaphore maintains a count to represent integer value, unlike mutex.
- Semaphores can perform Synchronization tasks when the counter is equal to 0 and the allocation of N resources when the center is greater than 1.

23. What is a spinlock?

Answer:

A spinlock is a lock which causes a thread trying to acquire it to simply wait in a loop ("spin") while repeatedly checking if the lock is available. Since the thread remains active but is not performing a useful task, the use of such a lock is a kind of busy waiting. Once acquired, spinlocks will usually be held until they are explicitly released, although in some implementations they may be automatically released if the thread being waited on (the one which holds the lock) blocks, or "goes to sleep".

24. What is a deadlock and how can you resolve it?

Answer:

Deadlock is a situation in which two or more processes cannot proceed because they are both waiting for the other to release some resources.

Possible solution: The best solution is to prevent deadlocks in the design – manage how requests for resources can be made in the system and how they are handled. The goal is to ensure that at least one of the necessary conditions for deadlock can never hold. A more costly solution is to dynamically consider every request and decides whether it is safe to grant it at a certain point.

A specific example of good design is to duplicate critical resources. Don't store critical information in one place and let multiple processes try to access them. Rather, deliver critical information to each interesting process.

Priority inversion: a situation where a low-priority task holds a resource that a higher-priority task is waiting for. This leads to deadlock as the low-priority task cannot be scheduled to release the lock, and the high-priority task can't continue without the lock on the resource.

Possible solutions: allow the low-priority task to temporarily take on the priority of the other task, enabling its scheduling and release of the lock. Another solution is prevention – make sure that higher priority tasks are never dependent on resources that can be held by lower priority tasks.

Note that a priority inversion is an example of deadlock.

25. What is priority Inversion?

Answer:

A high priority task (H) is blocked by a low priority task (L) because L has locked some resources needed by H, and L must wait for a medium priority task (M). This can be a problem if M takes a long time, this will cause H to miss a deadline. A possible solution is to have tasks inherit the maximum priority of any task that is waiting for them. In that case, L temporarily becomes a high priority until H can proceed, thus preventing M from running in place of H.   Priority inheritance is a putative solution.

Another solution is prevention – make sure that higher priority tasks are never dependent on resources that can be held by lower priority tasks.

26. How does the priority inheritance protocol work?

Answer:

When a low-priority task acquires a shared resource, the task continues running at its original priority level. If a high-priority task requests ownership of the shared resource, the low-priority task is hoisted above the requesting task. The low-priority task can then continue executing its critical section until it releases the resource.

Once the resource is released, the task is dropped back to its original low-priority level, permitting the high-priority task to use the resource it has just acquired.

27. For each of the following situations, discuss which shared-data protection mechanisms seem most likely and why?
    a. **Task M and Task N share an `int` array, and each often must update many elements in the array.**
    b. **Task P shares a single char variable with one of the Interrupt routines.**

    Answer:

Tasks M and N should probably use a semaphore. Since each of them must update many elements in the array, disabling Interrupts may keep Interrupts disabled for too long a period of time (obviously depending upon how fast your Interrupt routines need to respond). Task P, on the other hand, must disable Interrupts, since there is no other mechanism to deal with data that is shared with an Interrupt routine.

Scheduler

28. What type of scheduling is there in RTOS or Embedded OS?
    Answer:

Most embedded operating systems use pre-emptive scheduling. In pre-emptive scheduling, the higher priority task can Interrupt a running process and the Interrupted process will be resumed later.

29. What are the typical states of a task in an embedded OS?

Answer:

Whether it's a system task or an application task, at any time each task exists in one of a small number of states, including ready, running, or blocked. As the real-time embedded system runs, each task moves from one state to another, according to the logic of a simple finite state machine (FSM).

The figure below illustrates a typical FSM for task execution states, with brief descriptions of state transitions.

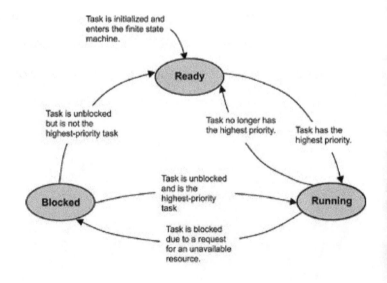

Although kernels can define task-state groupings differently, generally three main states are used in most typical preemptive-scheduling kernels, including:

- *Ready* state - the task is ready to run but cannot because a higher priority task is executing.
- *Blocked* state - the task has requested a resource that is not available, has requested to wait until some event occurs, or has delayed itself for some duration.
- *Running* state - the task is the highest priority task and is running.

Note that some commercial kernels may have different states.

30. Consider this statement:

"In a non-preemptive RTOS, tasks cannot 'Interrupt' one another: therefore, there are no data-sharing problems among tasks." Would you agree with this?

Answer:

This statement is true. The shared data problem arises when the CPU is switched away from one task while that task was using the shared data. Since this does not happen in a non-preemptive RTOS, there is no shared data problem among tasks. (Of course, if there is data shared between tasks and Interrupt routines, there is still a potential problem with that.)

Timers

31. What is a watchdog timer?

Answer:

The watchdog timer is a hardware timing device that is periodically reset by software. If the software crashes or hangs, the watchdog timer will expire, and the entire system will be reset automatically. The intention is to bring the system back from the hung state into normal operation.

The watchdog timer is a counter (usually a 16 bit) that resets the processor when it rolls over to zero.

32. What are the various uses of timers in an embedded system?

Answer:

Timers in the embedded system is used in multiple ways such as:

- Real-Time Clock (RTC) for the computer system
- Initiating an event after the preset time delay
- Initiating an event after the comparison of preset times
- Calculate the value in timer on any event
- Finding the time interval between two events

- Time slicing for different tasks
- Time-division multiplexing
- Setting up of various tasks in RTOS

Memory

33. How does the program memory areas in an embedded operating system?

Answer:

When a program is launched, the operating system creates and allocates a collection of memory area for the program to execute

- A code/text area that contains the process execution
- A stack area that holds local variables, return pointers, call stack
- A data area where the process stores its global or static variables data
- A BSS segment, that holds uninitialized data
- A heap area that holds dynamically allocated data

Stack
↑

↓
heap
.bss *(uninitialized data)*
.data *(initialized data)*
.text *(code)*

34. Reasonable design of memory management is to allocate three or four memory buffer pools, each with a different size of the buffer. What drawbacks can you see to this design compared to using malloc and free?

Answer:

Although one solution to using several memory buffer pools uses memory more efficiently than using just one pool, it is still not as effective as malloc and free. Any task that needs memory will have to select from one of a set of predetermined sizes, and some tasks will no doubt waste some of the memory that they have allocated. Further, you will have to decide ahead of time how many of each size of buffer your system will have. If the task goes after a buffer of a certain size, and the system has run out of buffers of that size, then the memory allocation will fail, even if there are plenty of other buffers of different sizes.

Embedded programming

35. What makes the code Re-entrant?

Answer:

A routine or a function is considered reentrant if it can safely call the function again before its previous invocation has been completed 9i.e. it can be safely executed concurrently). To be reentrant it must not any static/global data, call on functions in a non-atomic way, uses hardware in a non-atomic way, and mostly uses local variables.

36. What do you protect shared data?

Answer:

Shared data is protected using semaphores, disabling task switching, and bounding it with Interrupts (enabling/disabling) to execute a piece of code without Interruptions.

37. How does the debugger work?

Answer:

A debugger can start some process and debug it or attach itself to an existing process. It can single-step through the code, set breakpoints, and run to them, examine variable values and stack traces.

38. What is the difference between a hardware breakpoint vs. a software breakpoint?

Answer:

Hardware breakpoints are actually comparators, comparing the current PC with the address in the comparator (when enabled). Hardware breakpoints are the best solution when setting breakpoints.

Software breakpoints are in fact set by replacing the instruction to be break pointed with breakpoint instruction. The breakpoint instruction is present in most CPUs, and usually as short as the shortest instruction. Software breakpoints can easily be set if the program is located in RAM.

39. What is the need for an infinite loop in embedded systems?

Answer:

Embedded systems need infinite loops for repeatedly processing/monitoring the state of the program. One example could be the case of a program state continuously being checked for any exceptional errors that might just occur during run-time such as memory outage or divide by zero etc.,

```
While(Boolean True) OR for(;;);
{
//Code
}
```

For example, Customer care Telephone systems wherein a pre-recorded audio file are played in case the dialer is put on hold. Another example is a circuit that is responsible for indicating that a particular component is active/alive during its operation by means of LED's.

40. What is the stack overflow?

Answer:

If your program tries to access beyond the limit of the available stack memory then stack overflow occurs. In other words, you can say that a stack overflow occurs if the call stack pointer exceeds the stack boundary.

If stack overflow occurs, the program can crash or you can say that segmentation fault that is the result of the stack overflow.

41. What is the cause of the stack overflow?

Answer:

In the embedded application we have a little amount of stack memory as compare to the desktop application. So, we have to work on embedded applications very carefully either we can face the stack overflow issues that can be a cause of the application crash.

Here, I have mentioned some causes of unwanted use of the stack.

- Improper use of the recursive function.
- Passing to many arguments in the function.
- Passing a structure directly into a function.
- Nested function calls.
- Creating a huge size local array.

42. What are the start-up code steps?

Answer:

Start-up code for C programs usually consists of the following actions, performed in the order described:

- Disable all Interrupts.
- Copy any initialized data from ROM to RAM.
- Zero the uninitialized data area.
- Allocate space for and initialize the stack.
- Initialize the processor's stack pointer.
- Create and initialize the heap.
- Enable Interrupts.
- Call the main.

43. How to access the fixed memory location in embedded C?

Answer:

Let us see an example code to understand this concept. This question is one of the best questions of the embedded C interview question.

Suppose in an application, you need to access a fixed memory address. So, you need to follow the below steps, these are high-level steps.

```
//Memory address, you want to access
#define RW_FLAG 0x1FFF7800

//Pointer to access the Memory address
volatile uint32_t *flagAddress = NULL;

//variable to store the read value
uint32_t read Data = 0;

//Assign address to the pointer
flagAddress = (volatile uint32_t *)RW_FLAG;

//Read value from memory
*flagAddress = 12; // Write

//Write value to the memory
readData = * flagAddress;
```

44. What are the common causes of a segmentation fault in C?

Answer:

There are many reasons for the segmentation fault, here I am listing some common causes of the segmentation fault.

- Dereferencing NULL pointers.

- Tried to write read-only memory (such as code segment).

- Trying to access a nonexistent memory address (outside process's address space).

- Trying to access memory the program does not have rights to (such as kernel structures in process context).

- Sometimes dereferencing or assigning to an uninitialized pointer (because might point an invalid memory) can be the cause of the segmentation fault.

- Dereferencing the freed memory (after calling the free function) can also be caused by the segmentation fault.

- A stack overflow is also caused by the segmentation fault.

- A buffer overflow (try to access the array beyond the boundary) is also a cause of the segmentation fault.

45. What is the difference between Segmentation fault and Bus error?

Answer:

In the case of segmentation fault, SIGSEGV (11) signal is generated. Generally, a segmentation fault occurs when the program tries to access the memory to which it doesn't have access to.

Below I have mentioned some scenarios where SIGSEGV signal is generated.

- When trying to de-referencing a NULL pointer.
- Trying to access memory which is already de-allocated (trying to use dangling pointers).
- Using uninitialized pointer(wild pointer).
- Trying to access memory that the program doesn't own (e.g. trying to access an array element out of array bounds).

In case of a BUS error, SIGBUS (10) signal is generated. The Bus error issue occurs when a program tries to access an invalid memory or unaligned memory. The bus error comes rarely as compared to the segmentation fault.

Below I have mentioned some scenarios where SIGBUS signal is generated.

- Non-existent address.
- Unaligned access.
- Paging errors

46. Consider a system that controls the traffic lights as a major intersection.

It reads from sensors that notice the presence of cars and pedestrians, it has a timer, and it turns the lights red and green appropriately. What architecture might you use for such a system? Why?

Answer:

If all that the system has to do is to control the traffic lights, it is difficult to imagine that a round-robin architecture would not suffice. Controlling traffic lights does not require any complicated calculation, so even a slow microprocessor doing perhaps less than one million instructions per second should be able to get around its loop in a tiny fraction of a second, much faster than any required response to traffic lights. You might even be able to write this system without Interrupts because the microprocessor might be able to get around its loop quickly enough to poll sensors in the street that detect automobiles and buttons for pedestrians. However, to determine this you would need to know something about how the buttons and sensors work and how fast your microprocessor is. One question that you would certainly want to ask is "What else does this system have to do?" Another question that might be worth asking is how fast the microprocessor will be.

Embedded hardware

47. What are the mechanisms used to configure modern Systems-on-chips at reset?

   Answer:

   Pull-up registers on I/O or bus signals, configuration word in a flash. Examples are Pin direction, enable internal pull-up resistor, edge vs. level enablement of Interrupts.

48. How many wires are required to reliably implement TTL- like serial communication between two devices, and why?

   Answer:

   TTL-like serial communication is often used to interface small microcontroller-based devices to larger computer systems, either for general communication or for uploading firmware. This type of communication uses two wires, one for each direction, called TX (transmit) and RX (receive.) But there also needs to be a common electrical ground level shared between the devices, so the minimum number of wires to reliably implement TTL serial communication is three. (The requirement for the common electrical ground is also present in I2C and SPI.)

49. Why are 8-bit microcontrollers still used when 32-bit & 64-bit microcontrollers exist?

Answer:

The general reason is picking the right tool for the job. The three most common reasons are backward compatibility, price, and electrical power consumption. Backward compatibility is important when interfacing with existing infrastructure, especially in industrial environments, where in many cases, the electrical and operational constraints impact the choice of microcontrollers.

Generally, smaller microcontrollers (with narrower primary registers) are also cheaper. But they can contain a very large selection of peripherals and interfacing options, so they can be used in many situations that require advanced functionality but not high CPU speed.

Smaller microcontrollers also generally require less power to operate, which is especially important for IoT and battery-powered devices.

50. Mention what buses are used for communication in an embedded system?

Answer:

In an embedded system, the following buses are used for communication

- I2C: used for communication between multiple ICs
- CAN: used in automobiles with centrally controlled network
- USB: used for communication between CPU and devices like mouse, etc.
- While ISA, EISA, PCI are the standard buses for parallel communication being used in PCs & other network devices.

51. What is the difference between a microprocessor and a micro-controller?

Answer:

A microprocessor is a manager of resources (I/O, memory) which lie outside of its architecture. Micro-controllers have I/O, memory, etc. built into it and specifically designed for control applications.

52. What is a DMA and how does the DMA work?

Answer:

DMA is direct memory access which is a technique for transferring data from main memory to a device without passing it through the CPU. Systems that have DMA channels can transfer data to and from devices much more quickly than systems without a DMA channel can.

53. What is the difference between a driver and firmware?

Answer:

Device drivers are dependent on the operating system and hardware. A driver acts as a translator between the hardware device and the programs or operating systems on which the hardware is installed. Firmware is a software program permanently installed into a hardware device such as a keyboard, hard drive, BIOS, or video cards and is independent to operate the hardware accordingly. It draws power from the source on which it runs.

54. Does DMA deal with physical or virtual address?

Answer:

DMA deals with Physical addresses.

- Only when CPU accesses addresses it refers to MMU(Memory Management Unit) and MMU converts the Physical address to Virtual address.
- But DMA controller is a device which directly drives the data and address bus during data transfer. So, it is purely a physical address. (It never needs to go through MMU & Virtual addresses).
- That is why when writing the device drivers, the physical address of the data buffer has to be assigned to the DMA.

55. What are the main functions of a multiplexed address and a data bus?

Answer:

The memory bus is used to carry the address and the data from the processor to the memory so that it can be easily accessed by the devices. These buses carry the value of the data that has to be passed for proper functioning. The use of the technique "Time-division multiplexing" is used that allows the reading and writing of the data to be done from the same bus line. This requires lots of time to be given to the bus so that it can complete the read and write operation of the data in the memory. This is a very expensive process due to the data transfer technique that is used in between the processor and the memory. This also gives the concept of cache and provides algorithms to solve the problems occurring in 'read' and 'write' operations

56. What are the different types of buses used by embedded systems?

Answer:

Buses are used to pass the messages between different components of the system. The most common buses are as follows:

Memory Bus: it is related to the processor that is connected to the memory (RAM) using the data bus. This bus includes the collection of wires that are in series and runs parallel to each other to send the data from memory to the processor and vice versa.

Multiplexed Address/Data Bus: Multiplex data bus consists of the bus that can read and write in the memory but it decreases the performance due to the time consumed in reading and writing of the data in the memory.

De-multiplexed Bus: these consist of two wires on the same bus, where one wire consists of the address that needs to be passed, and the other one consists of the data that need to be passed from one to another. This is a faster method compared to others.

Input/output bus: it uses the multiplexing techniques to multiplex the same bus input and output signals. This creates the problem of having the deadlock due to slow processing of it.

57. Why the vast majority of high performance embedded systems use RISC & why?

Answer:

Below are some of the reasons RISC (Reduced instruction set computing) architecture is attractive for usage in embedded systems:

- RISC instructions operate at an individual cycle level and are very fast.
- Register usage is optimized and memory access is limited to store and load operations

- Instruction sets are simple, addressing modes are few leading to greater efficiency, compilers are optimized

58. What is a Raspberry Pi?

Answer:

Raspberry Pi is a credit card-sized computer that is capable of doing all operations like a conventional computer. But it also has other built-in features like onboard Wi-Fi, Bluetooth, and GPIO pins to communicate with other external Things.

59. What are GPIO Pins?

Answer:

GPIO stands for General Purpose Input and Output pins. It is capable of reading and writing data from development boards like Raspberry and Arduino to other Sensors, motors, actuators, etc.

60. What is a Thermocouple, and how does it work?

Answer:

A Thermocouple is an electrical device comprised of two different electrical conductors joined together to form an electrical junction at different temperatures. This junction is used to measure the temperature. When the junction experiences a temperature change as a result of the Thermoelectric effect, Thermocouple produces a temperature-dependent voltage, and this voltage is interpreted using Thermocouple across the junction to measure the temperature.

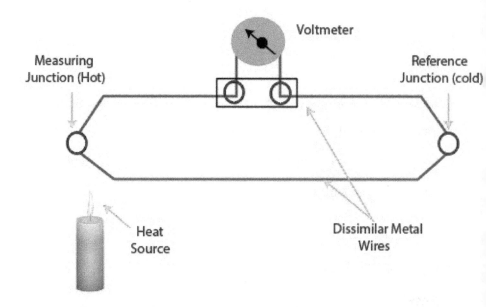

The thermocouple working principle based on three effects, discovered by Seebeck, Peltier, and Thomson.

Seeback Effect-The Seeback Effect states that when two different or unlike electrical conductors are joined together at a junction then an Emf is induced and the value of induced Emf is different for each electrical conductor.

Peltier Effect- Peltier Effect states that when two dissimilar conductors are joined together at a junction. An Emf induced in the circuit due to the temperature difference of the two electrical conductors.

Thomson Effect - Thomson Effect states that when two dissimilar or unlike electrical conductors are joined together at a junction. The potential induces within the circuit due to the temperature gradient across the entire length of the electrical conductors.

61. What is PWM (Pulse Width Modulation)?

Answer:

PWM (Pulse Width Modulation) or PDM (Pulse Duration Modulation) is a method for generating an analog signal via the digital source. PWM mainly consists of two different components that describe its operation and a frequency.

A "duty cycle" is defined as the number of times the signal is in ON state as what percentage of the total time it takes to complete one revolution.

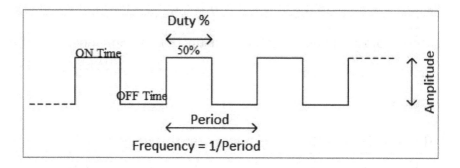

Frequency is defined as how much time taken by the PWM to complete one revolution.

- Frequency= 1/Time period
- Time Period= Time On+ Time Off

62. What is the difference between the I2c and SPI communication Protocols?

Answer:

In the embedded system, I2C and SPI both play an important role. Both communication protocols are the example of synchronous communication but still, both have some important differences.

The important difference between the I2C and SPI communication protocol.

- I2C supports half-duplex while SPI is full-duplex communication.
- I2C requires only two-wire for communication while SPI requires three or four-wire for communication (depends on requirement).

- I2C is slower as compared to the SPI communication.
- I2C draws more power than SPI.
- I2C is less susceptible to noise than SPI.
- I2C is cheaper to implement than the SPI communication protocol.
- I2C work on wire and logic and it has a pull-up resistor while there is no requirement of a pull-up resistor in case of the SPI.
- In I2C communication we get the acknowledgment bit after each byte, it is not supported by the SPI communication protocol.
- I2C ensures that data sent is received by the slave device while SPI does not verify that data is received correctly.
- I2C supports multi-master communication while multi-master communication is not supported by the SPI.

One great difference between I2C and SPI is that I2C supports multiple devices on the same bus without any additional select lines (work on the basis of device address) while SPI requires additional signal (slave select lines) lines to manage multiple devices on the same bus.

- I2C supports arbitration while SPI does not support the arbitration.
- I2C support the clock stretching while SPI does not support the clock stretching.

- I2C can be locked up by one device that fails to release the communication bus.
- I2C has some extra overhead due to start and stop bits.
- I2C is better for long-distance while SPI is better for the short distance.
- In the last I2C developed by NXP while SPI by Motorola.

63. What is the difference between Asynchronous and Synchronous Communication?

Answer:

There are the following differences between asynchronous and synchronous communication.

Asynchronous Communication	Synchronous Communication
There is no common clock signal between the sender and receivers.	Communication is done by a shared clock.
Sends 1 byte or character at a time.	Sends data in the form of blocks or frames.

Slow as compare to synchronous communication.	Fast as compare to asynchronous communication.
Overhead due to start and stop bit.	Less overhead.
Ability to communicate long distance.	Less as compared to asynchronous communication.
A start and stop bit used for data synchronization.	A shared clock is used for data synchronization.
Economical	Costly
RS232, RS485	I2C, SPI.

64. What is the difference between RS232 and RS485?

Answer:

The RS232 and RS485 is an old serial interface. Both serial interfaces are the standard for data communication.

Parameter	RS232	RS485
Line configuration	Single-ended	differential
Numbers of devices	1 transmitter 1 receiver	32 transmitters 32 receivers

Mode of operation	Simplex or full-duplex	Simplex or half-duplex
Maximum cable length	50 feet	4000 feet
Maximum data rate	20 Kbits/s	10 Mbits/s
signaling	unbalanced	balanced
Typical logic levels	+-5 ~ +-15V	+-1.5 ~ +-6V
Minimum receiver input impedance	3 ~ 7 K-ohm	12 K-ohm
Receiver sensitivity	+-3V	+-200mV
Parameter	RS232	RS485
Line configuration	Single-ended	differential

65. What is the difference between Bit Rate and Baud Rate?

Answer:

Bit Rate	Baud Rate
The bit rate is the number of bits per second.	Baud rate is the number of signal units per second.
It determines the number of bits traveled per second.	It determines how many times the state of a signal is changing.
Cannot determine the bandwidth.	It can determine how much bandwidth is required to send the signal.

This term generally used to describe the processor efficiency.	This term generally used to describe the data transmission over the channel.
Bit rate = baud rate x the number of bits per signal unit	Baud rate = bit rate / the number of bits per signal unit

66. What is the difference between Asynchronous and Synchronous Communication?

Answer:

There are the following differences between asynchronous and synchronous communication.

67. What is I2C (Inter-Integrated Circuit) communication?

Answer:

I2C is a serial communication protocol. It provides good support to the slow devices, for example, EEPROM, ADC, I2C LCD, and RTC, etc. It is not only used with the single board but also used with the other external components which have connected with boards through the cables.

I2C is basically a two-wire communication protocol. It uses only two-wire for communication. In which one wire is used for the data (SDA) and other wire is used for the clock (SCL).

In I2C, both buses are bidirectional, which means the master able to send and receive the data from the slave. The clock bus is controlled by the master but in some situations, the slave is also able to suppress the clock signal, but we will discuss it later.

Additionally, an I2C bus is used in various control architecture, for example, Sambas (System Management Bus), PMBus (Power Management Bus), IPMI (Intelligent Platform Management Interface), etc.

68. What is a bus arbitration?

Answer:

The arbitration is required in the case of a multi-master, where more than one master is trying to communicate with a slave simultaneously. In I2C arbitration is achieved by the SDA line.

Suppose two masters in the I2C bus are tried to communicate with a slave simultaneously then they will assert a start condition on the bus. The SCL clock of the I2c bus would be already synchronized by the wired and logic.

Example:

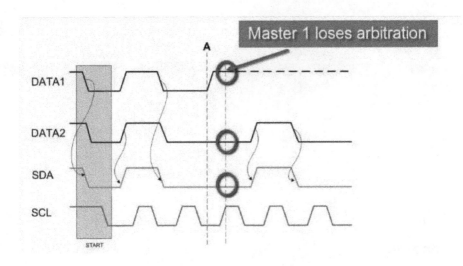

In the above case, everything will be good till the state of SDA line will same what is the masters driving on the bus. If any master sees that the state of SDA line differs, what is it driving then they will exit from the communication and lose their arbitration.

69. What is CAN bus?

Answer:

A Controller Area Network (CAN bus) is a robust vehicle bus standard designed to allow microcontrollers and devices to communicate with each other in applications without a host computer. It is a message-based protocol, designed originally for multiplex electrical wiring within automobiles to save on copper, but can also be used in many other contexts.

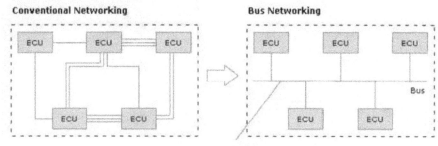

Conventional to CAN Network Transition

70. What is CSMA/CA and CSMA/CD in CAN Communication?

Answer:

CSMA (Carrier Sense Multiple Access) is used in transmission media access. If multiple ECUs are connected and sharing the same transmission medium to transfer its data. So, if they (multiple nodes) start transmission at the same time, then there is the possibility of collision and data corruption. CSMA introduces two concepts CSMA/CA and CSMA/CD to avoid this situation (collision and data corruption).

CSMA/CA (Carrier sense multiple access /collision avoidance) checks the state of the medium before sending it. It is applicable before starting the transmission. The node having CSMA/CA enabled features first check the transmission medium status before starting transmission. If the BUS is idle(free) then it will start transmission otherwise it will wait for the bus to be idle. In CAN this feature is introduced by the Arbitration concept.

CSMA/CD (Carrier Sense Multiple Access/Collision Detection) is applicable when the data transmission starts. A Node with CSMA/CD enabled feature detects the collision and stop the further data transmission. It will initiate data re-transmission. In CAN this feature is successfully implemented through Bit Monitoring feature of Transmitter node.

71. What is bit stuffing?

Answer:

Bit stuffing is the insertion of one or more bits into a transmission unit as a way to provide signaling information to a receiver. The receiver knows how to detect and remove or disregard the stuffed bits.

72. What does the timing diagram of a static RAM look like?

Answer:

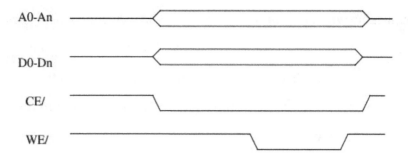

A0-An

D0-Dn

CE/

WE/

73. Design a circuit?

Assume that your system has two ROM chips and two RAM chips whose sizes and addresses are shown in the following table? Design the part of the circuit that takes the address lines and produces the chip enable signals for each of these four memory parts?

Answer:

	Size	Low Address	High Address
ROM	128 KB	0x00000	0x1ffff
ROM	128 KB	0x20000	0x3ffff
RAM	64 KB	0x80000	0x8ffff
RAM	64 KB	0x90000	0x9ffff

The first thing to notice in addressing this problem is that the highest-order address line, A19, is low in the addresses that belong to the ROM chips and high in the addresses that belong to the RAM chips.

Therefore, one or the other of the ROM chips should be enabled when A19 is low, and one or the other of the RAM chips should be enabled when A19 is high. Since the first of the ROM chips should be enabled as long as the address is less than Ox1ffff, it should, therefore, be enabled when A17 is low. The second ROM ship should be enabled when A17 is high. Similarly, the first RAM chip should be enabled when A16 is low, and the second should be enabled when A16 is high.

Assuming that the chip enable lines on both the ROM and the RAM chips are active low, one possible design that implements the comments in the above paragraph is as follows:

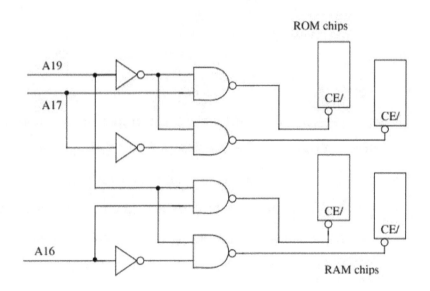

74. What are the (dis) advantages of edge-triggered & level-triggered Interrupts?

Answer:

The advantage of the edge-triggered Interrupt is that the device that is requesting the Interrupt need not continue signaling it; the microprocessor will recognize the edge of the signal even if it is just a pulse. The disadvantage is that if the device wants to signal two Interrupts, it must ensure that it stops asserting its Interrupt signal for a short time between the two so that the second Interrupt will cause an edge and be recognized by the microprocessor.

75. Why is FIFO useful for received bytes in a UART?

Answer:

A FIFO for received bytes is useful because it allows a certain number of bytes to pile up in the UART while the microprocessor is busy doing other things. A UART that has no FIFO can only remember one received byte at a time; this means that the microprocessor must read each byte from the UART before the next one is received. On a fast serial line, the microprocessor might not be able to keep up if it had to stop what it is doing and execute an Interrupt routine each time a single character came in. Even if the microprocessor could keep up, getting into and out of Interrupt routines would use up a lot of extra processor cycles. With a FIFO, the microprocessor can wait until several bytes have come in and then transfer them to the memory all at once.

76. How might you driver an LED if your microprocessor does not have any I/O pins?

Answer:

There are several ways to do this. One straightforward way to do it is to attach the LED to one of the outputs of a D flip flop. Attach the D input to the D0 data signal and build some circuitry that pulses the CLK input whenever the microprocessor writes to some particular address. Then the microprocessor can turn the LED on by writing the value 1 to the chosen address and turn it off by writing the value 0 (or vice versa, depending upon exactly how you acquire it up). Another popular way to control LEDs is to find some unused output on a UART (for example, RTS on a system that does not use RTS) and attach the LED to that. The microprocessor then instructs the UART whether to signal RTS high or low (typically by writing to a register within the UART) and thereby controls the LED.

Experience-based

77. What debugging tools did you use?

Answer:

Typically embedded system programmers use simulators, in-circuit emulators, JTAG debuggers, Software debuggers, LEDs, as well as serial or other communication ports. Some examples are as follows.

- Simulator – Simics from Windriver
- In-circuit emulators – ICE hardware provided by microcontroller vendor
- JTAG debugger – JTAG from Infineon, MIPS, Freescale, etc.
- Software debugger – Tornado from Windriver, gdb from GNU, Eclipse from opensource
- LEDs & communication ports – use LEDs to step through the code and print messages via serial or parallel communication ports

78. What type of source control software did you use?

Answer:

Embedded software is not the source control tools are the same. The popular ones include CVS, SVN, GIT, perforce, Bazaar, Clearcase, etc.

79. If a system crashes, what can do to figure out what happened?

Answer:

System crashes happen because of many reasons and are often difficult to debug. Below are few tools and techniques that are commonly used to get to the root cause

- Emulator/core dump/task threat/postmortem dump
- Debug data/exception handler data
- Checksum flash code

80. What does a map file contain?

Answer

The map file is generated by the linker and the format of the file will be different for each linker. However, for the most part, a map file is simply a table of symbols, their location, and their size. It will also have an overall summary of the memory usage for static data and code space. Code and data can be further categorized as read-only, read-write, etc.

Below is an example of a map file:

```
***********************************************************************
*** MODULE SUMMARY
***

    Module                        ro code  rw code  ro data  rw data
    ------                        -------  -------  -------  -------
C:\stash\SDK_2.2_QN908XCDK\boards\qn908xcdk\wireless_examples\bluetooth\heart_rate_
    ApplMain.o                    1 220             44       3 560
    FunctionLib.o                    78
    GPIO_Adapter.o                1 300             16          64
    GenericList.o                   184
    Keyboard.o                      484              8          32
    LED.o                           112              2           8
    MemManager.o                    292            612       2 524
    Messaging.o                      24|
    ModuleInfo.o                                    45           4
    PWR.o                           504                        15
    PWRLib.o                        472              1           5
```

81. When memory is a constraint, is it preferable to allocate memory statically or dynamically?

Answer:

It is preferable to use static memory because data overhead, CPU overhead, and memory fragmentation can be significant issues when using dynamic memory allocation.

82. What are the pro and cons of using a generic RTOS on a mid-range microcontroller?

Answer:

RTOSes can significantly ease the development of complex products, which can translate into faster development cycles. They often support compartmentalizing code into tasks, implement cross-task communication mechanisms, and commonly include abstractions ("drivers") for platform-specific hardware, which makes porting firmware to new hardware easier. Because of all that, they also introduce overhead in code size and CPU usage, which is not acceptable for all projects.

83. What are the characteristics of UART/RS-232, I2C, and SPI communication?

Answer:

Simple UART-based serial communication—with or without UART hardware—is the least demanding communications protocol to implement, but comes with severe limitations:

It's intended to connect only two devices.

It's asynchronous, meaning there's no explicit agreement about clock rates between the devices.

It's most commonly used at slow bit rates (up to 115,200 bps).

I2C can connect up to 127 devices on the same electrical bus, and each device is individually addressable. One of the devices, a master device, generates a clock signal shared by all the others, called slave devices. There is only one data wire, so all communication is unidirectional. (It's commonly used to communicate with sensors on a PCB, which often uses simple request-response protocols.)

The SPI bus is designed for fast, bidirectional communication with complex devices, which can involve cases such as transferring a large volume of data in bulk. With SPI, all devices share the data and clock wires, but there are also separate addressing wires which enable communication to and from specific devices.

84. What are C and C++ still widely supported in embedded firmware development?

Answer:

Hardware constraints, both for memory sizes and CPU speed, limit what can be done on embedded devices. C and C++ usually have very minimal overhead and are very "close to the hardware" in terms of abstractions offered to developers. This makes them suitable for even the smallest devices.

85. Are firmware and data embedded in microcontrollers generally safe from downloading, tampering, or hacking?

Answer:

No. Unless the microcontroller is specially constructed to offer countermeasures against firmware downloading and/or modification, any code and data uploaded to a microcontroller should be considered relatively easy to download and modify. (Such hardened microcontrollers are usually expensive.)

86. What are some of the commonly found errors in embedded systems?

Answer:

Some of the commonly found errors are:

- Damage of memory devices due to static discharges and transient current.

- Address line malfunctioning due to a short circuit
- Malfunctioning of Data lines
- Due to garbage or errors, some memory locations become inaccessible for storage
- Wrong insertion of memory devices into memory slots
- Wrong control of signals

87. Which one is better? Down_to_zero loop or Count_up_loops?

Answer:

Count down to zero loops are better because loop termination, comparison to zero are optimized by the compiler. Most processors have instruction for comparing to zero. So, there is no need to load the loop variable and the maximum value, subtract them, and then compare it to zero. All these make it efficient and better.

88. How to reduce function call overhead in ARM-based systems?

Answer:

Try to ensure that small functions take four or fewer arguments. These will not use the stack for argument passing. It will copy into registers.

- If a function needs more than four arguments, try to ensure that it does a significant amount of work, so that the cost of passing the stacked arguments is outweighed.

- Pass pointers to structures instead of passing the structure itself.
- Put related arguments in a structure and pass a pointer to the structure to functions. This will reduce the number of parameters and increase readability.
- Minimize the number of long parameters, as these take two argument words. This also applies to doubles if software floating-point is enabled.
- Avoid functions with a parameter that is passed partially in a register and partially on the stack (split-argument). This is not handled efficiently by the current compilers: all register arguments are pushed on the stack.
- Avoid functions with a variable number of parameters. Varargs functions.

89. What are the considerations when buying an embedded operating system?

Answer:

Some of the factors to consider should be as follows:
- Interrupt latency and context switching times
- Documentation providing for min, avg and maximum number of clock cycles by each system call
- Compatibility with various plugin devices
- Reliability of the operating systems

Technical questions (Coding)

C programming

General

90. Define the following: union, static, const, volatile, void *, extern, %, &, enum

   Answer:

   `union:`

   A union declaration specifies a set of variable values and, optionally, a tag naming the union. The variable values are called members of the union and can have different types. The storage associated with a union variable is the storage required for the largest member of the union. When a smaller member is stored, the union variable can contain unused memory space. All members are stored in the same memory space and start at the same address.

   `static:`

   The static keyword specifies that the variable has a static duration (it is allocated when the program begins and deallocated when the program ends) and initializes it to 0 unless another value is specified.

When modifying a variable or function at file scope, the static keyword specifies that the variable or function has internal linkage (its name is not visible from outside the file in which it is declared). A variable declared static in a function retains its state between calls to that function.

`const`:

Cannot be changed and optionally allows the linker to store this data in flash instead of RAM (in an embedded environment).

`volatile`:

Specifies that value may change outside of program control. Prevents code optimizer from removing references to this value. Example: memory-mapped I/O.

`void *`:

When used as a function return type, the function returns a pointer to a block of memory. The pointer needs to be type-cast to another type before it can be used. When used for the function parameter list, the function is supposed to know what type of data the void * pointer passed into the function is pointing to.

If a pointer's type is **void** *, the pointer can point to any variable that is not declared with the **const** or **volatile** keyword. A void pointer cannot be dereferenced unless it is cast to another type. A void pointer can be converted into any other type of data pointer.

extern:

The **extern** keyword declares a variable or function and specifies that it has external linkage (its name is visible from files other than the one in which it's defined). When modifying a variable, **extern** specifies that the variable has a static duration (it is allocated when the program begins and deallocated when the program ends). The variable or function may be defined in another source file, or later in the same file. In C++, when used with a string, **extern** specifies that the linkage conventions of another language are being used for the declarator(s). Declarations of variables and functions at file scope are external by default.

%:

The modulus (remainder from division) (%) operator yields the remainder given by the following expression, where e1 is the first operand and e2 is the second: e1 − (e1 / e2) * e2, where both operands are of integral types. Division by 0 in either a division or a modulus expression is undefined and causes a run-time error.

&:

The bitwise AND operator (&) compares each bit of the first operand to the corresponding bit of the second operand. If both bits are 1, the corresponding result bit is set to 1. Otherwise, the corresponding result bit is set to 0.

Also, the address of the operator. Returns the address of a variable.

enum:

The **enum** keyword specifies an enumerated type. An enumerated type is a user-defined type consisting of a set of named constants called enumerators. By default, the first enumerator has a value of 0, and each successive enumerator is one larger than the value of the previous one unless you explicitly specify a value for a particular enumerator. Enumerators need not have unique values. The name of each enumerator is treated as a constant and must be unique within the scope where the **enum** is defined. An enumerator can be promoted to an integer value. However, converting an integer to an enumerator requires an explicit cast, and the results are not defined.

91. What does the keyword const mean?

Answer:

Simply put, `const` means "read-only"

92. When should the register modifier be used? Does it really help?

Answer:

The register modifier hints the compiler that the variable will be heavily used and should be kept in the CPU's registers, if possible so that it can be accessed faster.

93. What do the following declarations mean?

```
const int a;
int const a;
const int *a;
int * const a;
int const * a const;
```

Answer:

```
const int a;         // const(read-only) integer
int const a;         // const(read-only) integer
const int *a;        //a is a pointer to a const integer
 int * const a;           // a is a const pointer to an
integer
                     // (integer modifiable, but not
                  the pointer)
int const * a const;     //a is a const pointer to a
                     const integer //(both not
                     modifiable)
```

94. How is a "union" different from a "struct" in "C"?

Answer:

Each member gets a separate memory location in a structure, whereas in a union, the total memory space is equivalent to the largest size member. All the members share the same memory space in a union

95. What is the difference between `(A && B)` and `(A & B)` ?

Answer:

`A&&B` is logical AND which returns the Boolean value **true** if both operands are **true** and return **false** otherwise. The operands are converted to Boolean prior to the evaluation, and the result is Boolean. The first operand is completely evaluated, and all side effects are completed before continuing the evaluation of the logical AND expression. The second operand is evaluated only if the first operand evaluates to true (nonzero). This evaluation eliminates needless evaluation of the second operand when the logical AND expression is false.

`A&B` is bitwise-AND which compares each bit of the first operand to the corresponding bit of the second operand. If both bits are 1, the corresponding result bit is set to 1. Otherwise, the corresponding result bit is set to 0.

Follow Up: If A=2 and B=1, what does each evaluate to? A&&B = true and A&B = 0

96. What is the advantage of a macro over a function?

Answer:

Macro gets to see the Compilation environment, so it can expand

___TIME__ __FILE__ #defines. It is expanded by the preprocessor. For

example, you can't do this without macros

  #define PRINT(EXPR) printf(#EXPR "=%d\n", EXPR)

  PRINT(5+6*7) // expands into printf("5+6*7=%d", 5+6*7);

You can define your mini-language with macros:

  #define strequal(A,B) (!strcmp(A,B))

Macros are necessary evils of life. The purists don't like them, but

without it, no real work gets done.

97. What is the difference between int (* comp)(char *, char *) and int
 *comp (char *, char *)?

Answer:

  ○ int (* comp) (char *, char *) is a pointer to a function named
   "comp" which takes two character pointers as arguments and
   returns an int.

o int * comp(char *, char *) is a function named "comp" which takes two character pointers as arguments and returns a pointer to an int.

98. What happens on the call stack when a subroutine is called?

Answer:

The caller preserves the current register context by pushing them onto the stack then pushes the parameters to be passed to the subroutine onto the stack. Finally, the "return address" (i.e. program counter where subroutine is called) is pushed on the stack.

The called subroutine then adjusts its stack frame registers and then allocates local variables declared within the called subroutine on the stack (essentially pushes them on the stack).

When the called subroutine returns, it will pass the return value via a register then adjust the stack pointer to the position when this routine was entered. Execution is resumed at the program location that was saved.

The caller then adjusts the stack pointer for the passed arguments and restores the register context by popping each one

99. What is the size of int?

Answer:

Most mainstream compilers match the size of the int to the size of the data bus. For example, if the bus size is 32 bit the size of the integer will be 4 bytes.

100. What are the typical sizes of int, char and float data type?

Answer:

The size of the char and int are always dependent on the underlying operating system or firmware. This is limited to the number of address lines in the address bus. The int usually takes up a value of 2 bytes or 4 bytes. The char can take up a space of 1 or 2 bytes. The float data type takes up a value of 4 bytes.

101. What is a void pointer in C?

Answer:

A void pointer in C is a pointer that is not associated with any data type. It is also called general-purpose pointer and it points to some data location in the storage means points to the address of a variable. One of the benefits of the void pointer is that it can be typecasted to a particular data type and used. Examples of functions in C that return void* are malloc() and calloc().

102.   In a function when do we use heap memory vs. stack memory?

Answer:

Heap memory is used for dynamic memory allocation and stack memory is used for static memory. Both are stored in the computer's RAM. Variables allocated on the stack are stored directly to the memory and access to this memory is very fast, and its allocation is dealt with when the program is compiled whereas dynamic memory can slow or fast.

103.   What happens when you overload the stack?

Answer:

When the stack is overloading the variable can fall outside of the call stack. This often causes the program to crash or freeze. Some operating systems give a stack overflow error that could be handled by an exception.

104.   Which data structure is used to perform recursion?

Answer:

A stack is the data structure that the operating system uses to keep track of recursive calls because stack operates in last in first out manner. In recursion, we generally transform the complex problem into a simpler subproblem, and using its solution we find the solution to a bigger problem.

105. How do you multiply a variable by 8 without using the multiplication operator?

Answer:

A computer represents every number in binary (i.e. power of 2). Therefore, we can represent a multiple as a sum of powers of 2 using a "Shift" operator

- For example, if we want to multiple a number(n) by 2, we write n<<1

- For example, if we want to multiple a number(n) by 8, C we write n<<3, and so on.

106. How can you check to see whether a symbol is defined?

Answer:

You can use the #ifdef and #ifndef preprocessor directives to check whether a symbol has been defined

(#ifdef) or whether it has not been defined (#ifndef)

107. How do you override a define macro?

Answer

You can use #undef preprocessor directive to undefine (override) a previously defined macro

108. How do you print an address?

Answer:

We can print the address of a variable or a function using the following specifiers %u, %p. %u prints address in decimal and %p prints in hex decimal form

109. How can you send an unlimited number of arguments to a function?

E.g. printf function can take any number of arguments?

Answer:

Using `va_list` variables in stdarg.h header file

Why should we assign NULL to the elements (pointer) after freeing them?

Answer

After a pointer has been freed, you can no longer use the pointed-to data. The pointer is said to "dangle"; it doesn't point at anything useful. If you "NULL out" or "zero out" a pointer immediately after freeing it, your program can no longer get in trouble by using that pointer.

110. What is the benefit of using an enum rather than a #define const?

Example:

```
enum error code
```

```
{
    OUT_OF_MEMORY,
    INSUFFICIENT_DISK_SPACE,
    FILE_NOT_FOUND
};
```

Vs.

```
#define    OUT_OF_MEMORY    0
#define    INSUFFICIENT_DISK_SPACE    1
#define    FILE_NOT_FOUND 2
```

Answer:

The use of an enumeration constant (enum) has many advantages over the symbolic constant style of #define. Below are some advantages

- o Enumerated constants are generated automatically by the compiler. Conversely, symbolic constants must be manually assigned values by the programmer
- o Enumerated constant method is that your programs are more readable, and this understood better by others
- o Some symbolic debuggers can print the value of the enumeration const but cannot do the same for symbolic constants

111. What is the difference between a string copy(strcpy) and a
memory copy (memcpy)?

Answer:

The strcopy() function is designed to work exclusively with strings.
It copies each byte of the source string to the destination string
and stop when the terminating null character has been moved.
On the other hand, the memcpy() function is designed to work
with any type of data because not all data ends with a null
character, you may provide the memcpy() function with the
number of bytes you want to copy from the source to the
destination.

112. What is loop unrolling?

Answer:

Small loops can be unrolled for higher performance, with the
disadvantage of increased code size. When a loop is unrolled, a
loop counter needs to be updated less often and fewer branches
are executed. If the loop iterates only a few times, it can be fully
unrolled, so that the loop overhead completely disappears.

Example:

```
int CountBitOne (uint n)  // without loop
unrolling
{
```

```
    int bits = 0;
      while (n != 0)
      {
          if (n & 1) bits++;
          n >> = 1;
      }
    return bits;
}


int CountBitOne(uint n) //with loop
unrolling
{
    int bits = 0;
      while (n != 0)
      {
      if (n & 1) bits++;
      if (n & 2) bits++;
      if (n & 4) bits++;
      if (n & 8) bits++;
      n >> = 4;
      }
  return bits;
}
```

113. What is the memory leak in C?

Answer:

A memory leak is a common and dangerous problem. It is a type of resource leak. In C language, a memory leak occurs when you allocate a block of memory using the memory management function and forget to release it.

```
int main ()
{
    char * pBuffer = malloc(sizeof(char) *
20);
        /* Do some work */
        return 0; /*Not freeing the allocated
memory*/
}
```

Note: once you allocate a memory than allocated memory does not allocate to another program or process until it gets free.

114. What are dangling pointers?

Answer:

Generally, daggling pointers arise when the referencing object is deleted or deallocated, without changing the value of the pointers. It creates the problem because the pointer is still pointing the memory that is not available. When the user tries to dereference the daggling pointers than it shows the undefined behavior and can be the cause of the segmentation fault.

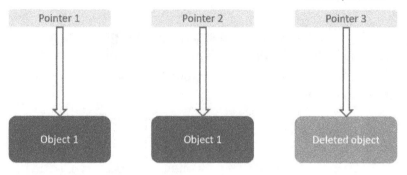

Dangling pointer because it is
pointing to the deallocated
memory location

| Pointer 1 | Pointer 2 | Pointer 3 |
| Object 1 | Object 1 | Deleted object |

Example:

```c
#include<stdio.h>
#include<stdlib.h>
int main()
{
    int *piData = NULL;
    //creating integer of size 10.
    piData = malloc(sizeof(int)* 10);
    //make sure piBuffer is valid or not
    if (piData == NULL)
    {
        // allocation failed, exit from the
program
        fprintf(stderr, "Out of memory!\n");
        exit(1);
    }
    //free the allocated memory
    free(piData);
    //piData is dangling pointer
    *piData = 10;
    printf("%d",*piData);
    return 0;
}
```

In simple words, we can say that a dangling pointer is a pointer that is not pointing to valid memory. So, if we access these pointers then the behavior of the program will undefine.

115.   What is the difference between pass-by-value and pass-by-reference in c?

Answer:

Pass by reference refers to passing the address of a variable given as a parameter. This is ideal when a calling subroutine must modify a variable not defined within its scope.

Pass by value refers to passing a copy of a variable given as a parameter. This is ideal when a calling subroutine does NOT want the variable passed as a parameter to be modified by the calling subroutine.

In 'C', all parameters are passed by value. To achieve the illusion of pass by reference, the programmer must explicitly pass the address (using &) of the variable.

Pass By Value:

- In this method, the value of the variable is passed. Changes made to formal will not affect the actual parameters.
- Different memory locations will be created for both variables.
- Here there will be a temporary variable created in the function stack which does not affect the original variable.

Pass By Reference :

- In Pass by reference, an address of the variable is passed to a function.
- Whatever changes made to the formal parameter will affect the value of actual parameters(a variable whose address is passed).
- Both formal and actual parameters shared the same memory location.
- it is useful when you required to returns more than 1 value.

116. Can do I define a structure without holes in it?

Answer:

By using a packed attribute shown in the example below:

```
struct ex {
INT8   source;
INT32 txSize;
INT32 datSize;
INT16 cmd;
} __attribute__ ((packed));
```

```
typedef struct ex PackedStruct;
```

117. Is this function reentrant?

```
int cErrors:
void vCountErrors (int cNewErrors)
cErrors += cNewErrors;
```

Answer:
This function is not reentrant (at least on most processors), because cErrors will be shared by any task that calls vCountErrors, and the use of cErrors is not atomic.

118. Is this function reentrant?

```
int strlen (char *p_sz)
{
int ilength;
ilength = 0:
while (*p_sz != '\0')
{
++ilength;
++p_sz;
return iLength;
}
}
```

Answer:
It is not possible to tell whether this function is reentrant. When it uses the value pointed to by p_sz, it may be accessing shared data. There is no way to tell this without seeing the code that calls strlen. In theory, there may be a problem. On the other hand, it is much more likely that different tasks will always pass p_sz

pointing to different strings, or that the strings passed to strlen are never changed while strlen is working on them. In these cases, strlen will work.

Find the output

119. What is the value of a at the end of each line?

```
int a = 5;
a = a+++a;
a = a+a++;
a = ++a+a;
a = ++a+a++;
```

Answer:

```
int a = 5;              Value of a = 5
a = a+++a;              Value of a = 11
a = a+a++;              Value of a = 11
a = ++a+a;              Value of a = 12
a = ++a+a++;       value of a = 13
```

120. What is the value of a, b and c at the end of each line?

```
int a=5;
int b=7;
int c;
c = a+++b;
c = a+b++;
c = ++a+b;
c = ++a+b++;
```

Answer:

```
int a=5;
int b=7;
int c;            Value of a = 5, b= c, c =
undefined
c = a+++b;        Value of a = 6, b = 7, c
= 12
c = a+b++;        Value of a = 5, b = 8, c
= 12
c = ++a+b;        Value of a = 6, b = 7, c
= 13
c = ++a+b++;   Value of a = 6, b = 8, c = 13
```

121. What is the value of z at the end of main()?

i. #inc
lude
<std
io.h
>

ii.

iii. int
func
tion
(int

```
         valu
         e)
iv.  {
 v.
         stat
         ic
         int
         temp
         = 1;
vi.
vii.
         temp
         +=
         valu
         e;
viii.
         retu
         rn
         temp
         ;
ix.  }
 x.
xi.  main
     ()
xii.  {
xiii.
         int
```

```
        x =
        1;
 xiv.
        int
        y =
        2;
  xv.
        int
        z =
        3;
xvi.
xvii.
        if
        (((x
        =
        func
        tion
        (x))
        ==
        2)||
        ((y
        =
        func
        tion
        (y))
        ==
        5))
```

```
xviii.
        {
xix.
            z =
            func
            tion
            (z);
    xx.
            }
    xxi.
    xxii.
            prin
            tf("
            Z =
            %d\n
            ",z)
            ;
    xxiii.  }
```

Answer:

The program prints: Z = 5

Note: once ((x = function(x)) == 2) evaluates to be "true" the other condition is not evaluated.

122.   What does the following code do?

```
int foo (char *s, char *t)
    {
    for ( ; *s == *t; s++; t++)
        if (*s == '\0')
            return 0;

    return (*s - *t);
    }
```

Answer:

The code fragment compares each sequential character until they are unequal or end of string character is reached.

If end of string is reached "0" is returned (meaning no difference between the strings).

If end of string is not reached (meaning the for loop conditional has failed), the difference between the two characters is returned.

The reason the function returns (*s - *t) is to facilitate sorting. A negative return value means the 1st string comes before the 2nd string and a positive value means the 1st string comes after the 2nd string and 0 means they are equal.

This function is strcmp().

123.   What does the following code fragment output and why?

```
        char *ptr;
            If (( ptr = (char *) malloc (0))
== NULL)
            else
            puts ("Got a NULL pointer")
        puts ("Got a valid pointer")
```

Answer:

Depending upon the compiler, `malloc (0)` may get a valid pointer, even memory is not allocated

124.   Which method if any, is preferred and why?

typedef is frequently used in C to declare synonyms for pre-existing data types. It is also possible to use the preprocessor to do something similar. For instance, consider the following code fragment:

```
#define dPS struct s *
typedef struct s * tPS;
```

The intent in both cases is to define dPS and tPS to be pointers to structures. Which method, if any, is preferred and why?

Answer:

typedef is preferred. For example:

```
dPS p1,p2;
tPS p3,p4;
```

The first expands to:

```
struct s * p1, p2;
```

which defines p1 to be a pointer to the structure and p2 to be an actual structure, which is probably not what you wanted. The second example correctly defines p3 and p4 to be pointers.

Identify errors

125. What is the difference between const *myPtr and char *const myPtr?

Answer:

Const char *myPtr is a non constant pointer to constant data; while char *const myPtr is a constant pointer to non-constant data.

126. Why does the assert fail?

```
xxxii.   void my_freem(int *v)
xxxiii.       {
xxxiv.        if (v != 0)
xxxv.         {
xxxvi.         free(v);
xxxvii.        v = 0;
xxxviii.       }
xxxix.         return;
xl.  }
```

xli.

xlii.

```
main()
```

xliii.   `{`

xliv.

```
void *ptr = (void *)malloc(1024);
```

xlv.

xlvi.

```
memset(ptr,0,512);
```

xlvii.

xlviii.

```
my_freemem((int *)ptr);
```

xlix.

```
assert(!ptr);
```

l.

li. `}`

Answer:

The ptr is passed by value so when v=0 inside my_freemem it only updates a copy not "ptr". To correct the code, modify my_freemem to take **v and then test if *v != 0 then update *v to 0.

127. What is wrong with this code?

```
void putlocks( char *NameCopy )
     {
          int length, i;
          char *c;

          length = strlen(NameCopy);
          if ((c = (char *)malloc(length)) ==
NULL)
               exit(1);
          strcpy(c, NameCopy);
          for (i = 0; i < length; i++)
          NameCopy[i] = tolower(c[i]);
     }
```

Answer:
A number of things are wrong:

- o   Lack of free (c);
- o   The malloc didn't allocate space for the NULL terminator and therefore the strcpy() call will copy 1 byte past the allocation.
- o   The whole function is wasteful of processing and memory resourced – the function can be performed in place using NameCopy[i] = tolower(NameCopy[i]) without a new copy of the string.

- o A comment might be made about exit() being used to abort the function – the suitability of this method would depend on the system requirements.

128. What is wrong with this code?

```
#include <stdlib.h>
 #include <stdio.h>

 main()
 {
    char *string1 = malloc(sizeof(char)*50);
    char *string2 = malloc(sizeof(char)*50);

    printf("\n\nPlease enter a label <less
than 50 characters>: ");
    scanf("%s", string2);
    string1 = string2;
    free(string2);
    free(string1);
    return 0;
    }
```

Answer:
string1 is now pointing to string2 and cannot be freed.

129. What is wrong with this code?

```
void putsLowcase( char *NameCopy )
    {
        int length, i;
        char *c;

        length = strlen(NameCopy);
        if ((c = (char *)malloc(length)) ==
  NULL)
```

```
            exit(1);
        strcpy(c, NameCopy);
        for (i = 0; i < length; i++)
        NameCopy[i] = tolower(c[i]);
    }
```

Answer:
The developer forgot to free the memory – free (c)

130. What is wrong with this code?

You have a situation where the phone needs to send power down indication message (pwr_dn_ind) to an external device before it powers off. The phone software runs on a real-time pre-emptive OS. Among a number of tasks, Task T1 handles the power down process, and Task T2 is responsible for sending the pwr_dn_ind message to the external device. You run into the situation where the phone powers off but the external device never gets the message.

Task T1:

```
void power_down()
    {
        SendMsgToT2(*ptr);  /*  T2 to send
pwr_dn_ind msg to ext dev */
        delay(2000);        /* Loop to delay 2000us
*/
/* It is sufficient for T2 to send pwr_dn_ind */
/* This delay consumes CPU time */
        power_down();       /* power down the phone
*/

    }
```

Task T2:

```
void os_task_T2()
{
    ReceiveMsg();       /* wait in a loop to
receive msg */
    SendMsgToExtDev(); /* send the pwr_dn_ind
msg to ext dev */
}
```

Answer:

T1's priority is higher than T2's. T2 won't get CPU time to run even if it gets the message

131.   What is the problem with the below code?

```
#define OS_TICK_FACTOR          0.25
#define REG_EV_VAL2TIMER_VAL(regev_val)
regev_val + OS_TICK_FACTOR * regev_val

#define REG_EVENT_EXPIRATION_VALUE(ticks,
max_interval)
    max_interval = (ticks +
0.5*REG_EV_VAL2TIMER_VAL(OS_TICK)));

    __Interrupt double timerevent   ()
    {

    test_interval =
REG_EVENT_EXPIRATION_VALUE(5,18.5);
```

```
    printf("\ntest_interval = %f",
test_interval);
    return tickstatus;
    }
```

Answer:

Below are some problems with the above code:

- o   OS_TICK is undefined

- o   ambiguous way to use the second define
  REG_EV_VAL2TIMER_VAL, need to have an enclosing
  bracket on the right-hand side

- o   Printing a value in ISR takes a lot of time/reentrancy issues
  ... a means of asking more questions on this topic

- o   returning from an ISR

132.   What is wrong with the following code fragment?

```
        unsigned int zero = 0;
        unsigned int compzero = 0xFFFF; /* 1's
complent of zero */
```

Answer:

On machines where an int is not 16 bits, this will be incorrect. The
correct code is

```
        unsigned int compzero = ~0;
```


133.   What is wrong with this Interrupt routine ?

```
__Interrupt double calculate_area (double
radius){
        Double area = PI * radius * radius;
        printf ("\n area = %f", area);
```

```
      Return area;
}
```

Answer:

Few issues with the Interrupt service routine (ISR)

- o ISRs cannot return a value
- o ISTs cannot be passed parameters
- o On many processors, floating-point (double) operations are not necessarily re-entrant and sometimes using floating-point are not allowed
- o Printf often has problems and is not reentrant and sometimes cannot handle causing it to or hang/freeze the system

134. Where to use semaphores in the following code to make the function reentrant?

```
static int iValue;
int iFixValue (int iParm)
{
        int iTemp;

        iTemp = iValue;
        iTemp += iParm * 17;

        if (iTemp > 4922)
        iTemp = iParm;
        iValue = iTemp;

        iParm = iTemp + 179;
        if (iParm < 2000)
        return 1;
```

```
        else
        return 0;
    }
```

Answer:

The answer is as shown below. Note that all of the time that

iFixValue uses iTemp as a temporary value to modify iValue

(which is shared by all of the tasks that call iFixValue), it must be

protected by a semaphore.

```
static int iValue;
int iFixValue (int iParm)
{
    int iTemp;
    OSSemGet (SEMAPHORE); /* Get it
here */

    iTemp = iValue;
    iTemp += iParm * 17;

    if (iTemp > 4922)
    iTemp = iParm;
    iValue = iTemp;

    OSSemGive (SEMAPHORE); /* Release
it here. */

    iParm = iTemp + 179;
    if (iParm < 2000)
    return 1;
    else
    return 0;
}
```

Bit manipulation

135.   Write a code snippet to swap endian?

Answer:

The following code converts little-endian code to big-endian and vice versa

```
uint32_t num = 0x12345678;
uint32_t result =
    ((num & 0x000000FF) << 16) |
    ((num & 0x0000FF00) << 8) |
    ((num & 0x00FF0000) >> 8) |
    ((num & 0xFF000000) >> 16);

printf("%0x\n", result);
```

136.   Embedded systems always require the user to manipulate bits in registers or variables.

Given n integer variable a, write two code fragments. The first should set bit 3 of a. the second should clear bit 3 of a. In both cases, the remaining bits should be unmodified?
Answer:

```
#define BIT3 (0x1 <<3)

static int a;
void set_bit3(void) {
    a|= BIT3;
 }

void clear_bit3(void) {
    a&= ~BIT3;
```

```
    }
```

137.   Set an integer variable at the absolute address 0x6789 to the value
        0xaabb?

Answer:

Ideally you should write:
```
    int *ptr;
    ptr = (int*) 0x6789;
    *ptr = 0xaabb;
```

However, most commonly embedded programmers write like
this:
```
    *(int *const) (0x6789) = 0xaabb;
```

Both the above answers are correct.

138.   Count set bits in a number.

Answer

Not-optimized:
```
int CountSetBits (int Num) {
    for (int count =0; Num; num >>=1)
    {
        If (Num & 1) count ++;
    }
    return count;
}
```
Optimized:
```
int countsetBits (int Num) {
    for (int count = 0; Num; count++)
    {
        Num &= Num -1;
    }
```

```
    }
```

139.   How to toggle a particular bit in C?

Answer:

```
int main(int argc, char *argv[])
{
    unsigned char cData=0xF8;
    int iPos =0;
     scanf("%d",&iPos);

    //toggle the nth bit.
    cData ^= 1<<iPos;

    printf("%d",iPos);

    return 0;
}
```

140.   Write the macros to set, clear, toggle, and check the bit of a given integer?

Answer

See the below macros

```
#define SET_BIT(value, pos) value |= (1U<< pos)
#define CLEAR_BIT(value, pos) value &= ~(1U<< pos)
#define TOGGLE_BIT(value, pos) value ^= (1U<< pos)
#define CHECK_BIT_IS_SET_OR_NOT(value, pos) value & (1U<< pos)
```

141. Write MACRO to swap the bytes in 32bit Integer Variable?

Answer:
See the macro below for the answer:

```
#define SWAP_BYTES(u32Value)  ((u32Value &
0x000000FF) << 24)\
|((u32Value & 0x0000FF00) << 8) \
|((u32Value & 0x00FF0000) >> 8) \
|((u32Value & 0xFF000000) >> 24)
```

Write code

142. Write the MIN macro that is, a macro that takes two arguments and returns the smaller of the two arguments?

Answer:
```
#define MIN (A,B)     ( (A) <= (B) > (A) : (B)
)
```

143. How do you create an infinite loop in embedded C?

Answer:
There are several solutions to this questions. Here are couple
- `while( 1 ) { }`
- `for ( ;; ) { }`

144. Using the variable a, give the definitions for the following:

a) An integer

b) A pointer to an integer
c) A pointer to a pointer to an integer
d) An array of 10 integers
e) An array of 10 pointers to integers
f) A pointer to an array of 10 integers
g) A pointer to a function that takes an integer as an argument and returns an integer
h) An array of ten pointers to functions that take an integer argument and return an
integer

Answer:
```
a) int a; // An integer
b) int *a; // A pointer to an integer
c) int **a; // A pointer to a pointer to an
integer
d) int a[10]; // An array of 10 integers
e) int *a[10]; // An array of 10 pointers to
integers
f) int (*a)[10]; // A pointer to an array of
10 integers
g) int (*a)(int); // A pointer to a function
a that takes an integer argument and returns
an integer
h) int (*a[10])(int); // An array of 10
pointers to functions that take an integer
argument and return an integer
```

145.   Write your own string copy function?

Answer:
```
char* my_strcopy(char*destination, const
char* source) {
  while( (*destination++ = *source++);
return destination;
}
```

146. Write your own memory copy function?

Answer:
```
void *memcpy (void *dst, void *src, size_t
len) {
    For(i=0; i<len; i++) {
        *dst++ = *src++;
    }
}
```

147. Write your own swap function which exchanges the values of two integers and the swap caller?

Answer:

Method 1:

```
void swap(int*a, int* b) {
  int temp;
  temp = *a;
  *a = *b;
  *b = temp;
}

void swapCaller() {
  Int x = 1;
  Int y = 2;
  Swap (&x, &y); // user & to pass pointers
to the int values
}
```

Method 2:

```
int main()
{
    int a = 10, b = 5;
    // algo to swap 'a' and 'b'
    a = a ^ b;   // a becomes (a ^ b)
```

```
    b = a ^ b;   // b = (a ^ b ^ b), b
becomes a
    a = a ^ b;   // a = (a ^ b ^ a), a
becomes b
    printf("After Swap value of: a = %d, b =
%d\n\n", a, b);
    return 0;
}
```

148.   Write a function to take a pointer to a singly linked list

as a parameter and return a pointer to a stack. Allocate memory
for and create a structure for stack and deallocate memory for
the list?
Answer:

```
char *myStackPtr, *myStackPtrStart;
typedef struct {char data; struct myList
*next;} myList;

        char *ConvertListToStack (myList
*listPtr)
        {
            int listSize=0, i;
            myList *listPtrStart;

            listPtrStart = listPtr;

            while(listPtr->next != 0)

            {
                listSize++;
                listPtr = listPtr->next;
                        }

            myStackPtr =
malloc(listSize*sizeof(char));
            myStackPtrStart = myStackPtr;
            listPtr = listPtrStart;
```

```
for (i=0;i<listSize;i++)
{
    *myStackPtr++ = listPtr->data;
    listPtr = listPtr->next;
}
free (listPtrStart);
return(myStackPtrStart);
}
```

149. Write your own integer to string conversion program?

Answer:

```
/* itoa:   convert n to characters in s */
 void itoa(int n, char s[])
 {
     int i, sign;

     if ((sign = n) < 0)   /* record sign */
         n = -n;                 /* make n positive
*/
     i = 0;
     do {          /* generate digits in
reverse order */
         s[i++] = n % 10 + '0';    /* get
next digit */
     } while ((n /= 10) > 0);      /* delete
it */
     if (sign < 0)
         s[i++] = '-';
     s[i] = '\0';
     reverse(s);
 }


#include <string.h>
```

```
/* reverse:  reverse string s in place */
  void reverse(char s[])
  {
      int i, j;
      char c;
       for (i = 0, j = strlen(s)-1; i<j; i++,
j--) {
          c = s[i];
          s[i] = s[j];
          s[j] = c;
      }
  }
```

150.   Reverse a singly linked list?

Answer:

```
Note * ReverseList ( Node ** List)
{
     Node *temp1 = *List;
     Node * temp2  = NULL;
     Node       * temp3  = NULL;

     While (temp1)
     {
          *List = temp1;        //set the head
to last note
          temp2 = temp1->pNext;    //save
the next ptr in temp2
          temp1->pNext = temp3; //change
next to previous
          temp3 = temp1;
          temp1 = temp2;
     }
     return *List;

}
```

151. Delete a node in double linked list?

Answer:

```
void deleteNode (node *n)
{
        node *np = n->prev;
        node *nn = n->next;
        np->next = n->next;
        nn->prev = n->prev;
        delete n;
}
```

152. Reverse a string

Answer

```
void reverseString (char *string)
{
        char *Begin = String;
        char *End = String + strlen (String) -
1;
        char TempChar = '\0';

        while (Begin < End)
        {
                Tempchar = *Begin;
                *Begin = *End;
                *End = TempChar;
                Begin++;
                End--;
        }
}
```

153. Write a function to Insert a node a sorted linked list?

Answer:

```
void sortedInsert (Node 8head, Node
*newNode)
{
        Node *current = head;
        //traverse the list until you find
item bigger
        //then the new node value

        While (current != NULL && current -
>data < newNode->data)
          {
              current = current ->next;
          }

        // insert the new node before the big
item

        newNode->next = current-<next;
        current = newNode;
}
```

154.   Write a function to Convert a string to upper case?

Answer:

```
void Toupper (char * S)
{
  While ( *S !=0)
    {
     *S = (*S  >=  'a'  &&  *S  <=  'z')  ?
(*S-'a'  +  'A'): *S;
      S++;
    }
}
```

155. Write a function to find the factorial of a number?

Answer:

```
int Factorial ( int Num) // recursive
version
{
        If (num > 0)
            return Num * Factorial (Num -1);
        else
        return 1;


}

int Factorial (int Num) //iterative version
{
        int I;
        int result = 1;

        for (I=num; I >0; I++)
        {
            Result = result * I;
        }

        return result;
}
```

156. Write a function to get Fibonacci number?

Answer:

```
int fib (n) //recursive version
{
        if (n < 2)
            return 1;
        else
            return fib (n-1) + fib 9n-2);
}
```

```
int fib (n) // iterative version
{
        int f1 = 1,  f2 =1;

        if ( n < 2 )
            return 1;
        for ( i =1; i< n; i++)
        {
            f = f1 + f2;
            f1 = f2;
            f = f1;
        }
        Return f;

}
```

157. Write a function that finds the last instance of a character in a string?

Answer:

```
char *lastchar (char* String, char ch)
{
        char *pStr = NULL;

        //traverse the entire string

        while ( *String++ != NULL)
        {
            If (*String == ch)
                pStr = String;
        }
        return pStr;
}
```

C++ programming

General

158. What is a friend function? Can we access the private member of the friend?

    Answer:

    A friend function of a class is defined outside that class scope but it has the right to access all private and protected member of the class. Even though the prototypes for friend functions appear in a class definition. Friends are not member functions.

    t can be invoked like a normal function without using the object. It cannot access the member names directly and has to use an object name and dot membership operator with the member name. It can be declared either in the private or the public part.

159. What is a copy constructor?

    Answer:

    A copy constructor is a member function that initializes an object using another object of the same class.

Syntax of copy constructor:

```
ClassName (const ClassName &old_obj);
```

160.   When are copy constructors called in C++?

Answer:

There are some possible situation when copy constructor called in C++,

- When an object of the class is returned by value.
- When an object of the class is passed (to a function) by value as an argument.
- When an object is constructed based on another object of the same class.
- When the compiler generates a temporary object.

161.   Why copy constructor takes the parameter as a reference in C++?

Answer:

A copy constructor is called when an object is passed by value. The copy constructor itself is a function. So, if we pass an argument by value in a copy constructor, a call to copy constructor would be made to call copy constructor which becomes a non-terminating chain of calls. Therefore, the compiler doesn't allow parameters to be passed by value.

162. Why copy constructor argument should be const in C++?

Answer:

There are some important reasons to use const in the copy constructor.

- `const` keyword avoids accidental changes.
- You would like to be able to create a copy of the const objects. But if you're not passing your argument with a const qualifier, then you can't create copies of const objects.
- You couldn't create copies from temporary reference, because temporary objects value, and can't be bound to reference to non-const.

163. What is the difference between copy constructor & assignment operator?

Answer:

A copy constructor constructs a new object by using the content of the argument object. An overloaded assignment operator assigns the contents of an existing object to another existing object of the same class.

Copy constructor is one that has only one argument, which is a reference to the same type as the constructor. The compiler invokes a copy constructor whenever it needs to make a copy of the object, for example, to pass an argument by value. If you do not provide a copy constructor, the compiler creates a member-by-member copy constructor for you.

Overloaded assignment operators that take arguments of other classes, but that behavior is usually implemented with implicit conversion constructors. If you do not provide an overloaded assignment operator for the class, the compiler creates a default member-by-member assignment operator.

164.   What is destructor in C++? When is the destructor called?

Answer:

A destructor is a member function that destructs or deletes an object.

A destructor function is called automatically when the object goes out of scope:

- At the function ends.
- When the program ends.
- A block containing local variables ends.

- When the delete operator is called.

165. Distinguish between shallow copy and deep copy?

Answer:

Shallow copies duplicate as little as possible. A shallow copy of a collection is a copy of the collection structure, not the elements. With a shallow copy, two collections now share the individual elements.

Deep copies duplicate everything. A deep copy of a collection is two collections with all of the elements in the original collection duplicated.

166. Is it possible to overload the destructor of the class?

Answer:

No, we cannot overload the destructor of the class.

167. What do you mean by pure virtual function?

Answer:

A pure virtual member function is a member function that the base class forces derived classes to provide. Normally these member functions have no implementation. Pure virtual functions are equated to zero

168. What is a virtual function? Why are there no virtual constructors but there are virtual destructors in C++?

Answer:

A virtual function is a member function that is declared within a base class and is re-defined (overridden) by a derived class. When you refer to a derived class object using a pointer or a reference to the base class, you can call a virtual function for that object and execute the derived class's version of the function.

- Virtual functions ensure that the correct function is called for an object, regardless of the type of reference (or pointer) used for function call.
- They are mainly used to achieve Runtime polymorphism
- Functions are declared with a virtual keyword in base class.
- The resolving of function call is done at Run-time.

In C++, the constructor cannot be virtual because when the constructor of a class is executed there is no virtual table in the memory, it means no virtual pointer defined yet. So, the constructors should always be non-virtual

169. Can we have a virtual destructor in C++? When to use virtual destructors?

Answer:

Yes, the destructor could be virtual in C++.

We can use virtual destructors when we will delete an object of the derived class using a pointer to the base class that has non-virtual destructor a results in undefined behavior.

170. What is "this" pointer?

Answer:

The "this" pointer is a pointer accessible only within the member functions of a class, struct, or union type. It points to the object for which the member function is called. Static member functions do not have this pointer. When a non-static member function is called for an object, the address of the object is passed as a hidden argument to the function.

An object's this pointer isn't part of the object itself. It's not reflected in the result of a sizeof statement on the object.

171. What is a namespace?

Answer:

A namespace is a declarative region that provides a scope to the identifiers (the names of types, functions, variables, etc) inside it. Namespaces are used to organize code into logical groups and to prevent name collisions that can occur especially when your codebase includes multiple libraries.

Example:

```
namespace Name_namespace

    {

        named_entities

    }
```

172. What is function overloading in C++?

Answer:

With the C++ language, you can overload functions and operators. A function Overloading is a common way of implementing polymorphism. An Overloading is a practice of supplying more than one definition for a given function name in the same scope. A user can implement function overloading by defining two or more functions in a class sharing the same name. C++ can distinguish the methods with different method signatures (types and number of arguments in the argument list).

Note: You cannot overload function declarations that differ only by return type.

173. What is Overriding?

Answer:

Overriding a method means that replacing a function functionality in child class. To imply overriding functionality we need parent and child classes. In the child class, you define the same method signature as one defined in the parent class.

In simple words, when the base class and child class have member functions with the same name, same return type, and same parameter list, then it is said to be function overriding.

Condition for the function overriding is:

- Must have the same method name.
- Must have the same data type.
- Must have the same argument list.

174. How do you call a C module within a C++ module?

Answer:

By using the `extern "C"` linkage specification around the C function declarations.

Example:

```
// C++ code
    extern "C" void f(int); // one way

    extern "C" {      // another way
        int gg(double);
        double hh();
    };

    void cplusplus_function(int i,
double d)
    {
        ff(i);
        int ii = gg(d);
        double dd = hh();
        // ...
    }
```

175. What is name mangling? And why do C++ compilers need it?

Answer:

Name mangling is the rule according to which C++ changes function's name into function signature before passing that function to a linker. This is how the linker differentiates between different functions with the same name

176. What is a dangling pointer?

Answer:

A dangling pointer arises when you use the address of an object after its lifetime is over. This may occur in situations like returning addresses of the automatic variables from a function or using the address of the memory block after it is freed.

177. What is a memory leak?

Answer:

Memory which has no pointer pointing to it and there is no way to delete or reuse this memory(object), it causes a Memory leak.

```
    {
            *b = new base();
    }
```

Out of this scope b no longer exists, but the memory it was pointing to was not deleted. The pointer by itself was destroyed when it went out of scope.

178. What is inline function?

Answer:

The inline keyword tells the compiler to substitute the code within the function definition for every instance of a function call. However, substitution occurs only at the compiler's discretion. For example, the compiler does not inline a function if its address is taken or if it is too large to incline

179. What are the differences between a struct in C and C++?

Answer:

In C++ a struct is similar to a class except for default access specifier. In C we have to include the struct keyword when declaring struct. In C++ we do not have to

180. What is The Order of Calling for The Constructors and Destructors in Case of Objects of Inherited Classes?

Answer :

The constructors are called with base class first order and the destructors are called in the child's first order. That is, if we have 2 levels of inheritance A (base)-> B (inherit 1)-> C (inherit 2) then the constructor A is called first followed by B and C. The C destructor is called first followed by B and A.

181. Explain the order of constructor and destructor calls in case of multiple inheritance?

Answer:

Constructors are top-down and destructors are bottom-up. For example:

- in parent's constructor
- in child's constructor
- in grandchild's constructor
- in grandchild's destructor
- in child's destructor
- in parent's destructor

182. What is name mangling? Provide an example?

Answer:

C++ supports function overloading, i.e., there can be more than one function with the same name and differences in parameters. C++ compiler distinguishes between different functions when it generates object code – it changes names by adding information about arguments. This technique of adding additional information to function names is called Name Mangling.

Example:

A single C++ translation unit might define two functions named f():

```
int   f (void) { return 1; }
int   f (int)  { return 0; }
void g (void) { int i = f(), j = f(0); }
```

These are distinct functions, with no relation to each other apart from the name. The C++ compiler therefore will encode the type information in the symbol name, the result being something resembling:

```
int    __f_v (void) { return 1; }
int    __f_i (int)  { return 0; }
void __g_v (void) { int i = __f_v(), j =
__f_i(0); }
```

Even though its name is unique, g() is still mangled: name mangling applies to all symbols.

183.   Why is the size of an empty class not zero in C++?

Answer:

The standard does not allow objects of size 0 since that would make it possible for two distinct objects to have the same memory address. That's why even empty classes must have a size of (at least) 1 byte.

```
#include<iostream>
using namespace std;
class Demo {};
int main()
{
    cout << sizeof(Demo);
    return 0;
}
// Output will be 1
```

184.   What is the difference between a C++ struct and C++ class?

Answer:

C++ struct has all the features of the class. The only differences are that C++ struct defaults to public member access and public base class inheritance, and a class defaults to the private access specified and private base-class inheritance.

Let see two examples

```cpp
#include <iostream>
using namespace std;
class Test
{
    int x; // x is private
};
int main()
{
    Test t;
    tax = 20; // compiler error because x is
private
    return 0;
}
```
Output: Error: 'int Test::x' is private

```cpp
#include <iostream>
using namespace std;
struct Test
{
    int x; // x is private
};
int main()
{
    Test t;
```

```
    t.x = 20; // compiler error because x is
private
        cout << t.x;
        return 0;
    }
```
Output: 20

185.   What is encapsulation?

Answer:

Containing and hiding Information about an object, such as internal
data structures and code. Encapsulation isolates the internal
complexity of an object's operation from the rest of the application.
For example, a client component asking for net revenue from a
business object need not know the data's origin.

186.   What Is Inheritance?

Answer:

Inheritance allows us to define a class that inherits all the methods
and attributes from another class. The class that inherits from
another class is called a derived class or child class. The class from
which we are inheriting is called parent class or base class.

Bit manipulation

187.   Write a function to display an integer in a binary format?

Answer:

```
void displayBits( unsigned value ) {
    const int SHIFT = 8 * sizeof( unsigned ) -
1;
    const unsigned MASK = 1<< SHIFT;
    cout << setw(10 ) << value << " = ";
    for ( unsigned i = 1; i <= SHIFT + 1; i++
)
        {
            cout << ( value & MASK ? '1' : '0' );
            value <<= 1;
        if ( i % 8 == 0 ) // output a space after
bits
        cout << ' ';
        }
    cout << endl;
}
```

You can also do the same using divide by 2, until the number is greater than 0 and then print it in the reverse order.

Advanced topics

Compilers & loaders

188. What is a compiler?

Answer:

A compiler is a program that takes source code as an input and converts it into an object code. During the compilation process, the source codes go through lexical analysis, parsing, and intermediate code generation which is then optimized to give final output as an object code.

189. What is a loader?

Answer:

A loader is a program routine that copies a program into memory for execution. i.e. it loads programs into main memory from the storage device (e.g. hard disk)

190. What is a linker?

Answer:

A linker is a utility program that links a compiled or assembled program to a particular environment. Also known as a "link editor," the linker unites references between program modules and libraries of subroutines. Its output is a load module, which is executable code ready to run on the computer.

191.   Define a Symbol Table?

Answer :

A symbol table is a data structure containing a record for each identifier, with fields for the attributes of the identifier. The data structure allows us to find the record for each identifier quickly and to store or retrieve data from that record quickly.

Whenever an identifier is detected by a lexical analyzer, it is entered into the symbol table. The attributes of an identifier cannot be determined by the lexical analyzer.

192.   What is a cross compiler?

Answer:

A cross-assembler is an assembler that runs on a computer with one type of processor but generates machine code for a different type of processor. For example, if we use a PC with the 8086 compatible machine language to generate machine code for the 8085 processor, we need a cross-assembler program that runs on the PC compatible machine but generates the machine code for 8085 mnemonics. It takes assembly language as input and gives machine language as output.

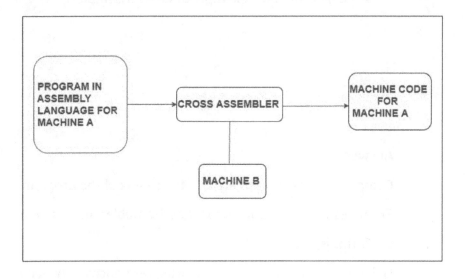

In the above block diagram, we can see that there is an assembler which is running on Machine B but converting the assembly code of Machine A to machine code, this assembler is Cross-assembler.

Features of Cross-Assembler :

- Cross-assembler is used to convert assembly language into binary machine code.
- Cross-assemblers are also used to develop a program which will run on a game console and other small electronic systems which are not able to run a development environment on their own.

- Cross-assembler can be used to give speed development on a low powered system.
- C 64 is the best example of Cross-assembler.

193. Give examples for : compile-time error, link-time error and run time error?

Answer:

Compile-time error is an error in the syntax of the program. Examples would be using undeclared variables, mismatch of parenthesis, etc.

Link time error is an error in resolving references between object modules – modules that were generated by the compiler. An example would be a missing implementation of a function that is used by at least one module.

In both cases above a downloadable (or executable) file was not generated.

Run time error is an error that occurs once the program is executed. The most common example is a divide by zero error. Other examples are memory allocation failure, use of null pointer, etc

194. What is the difference between static linking and dynamic linking?

Answer:

Static linking is done at the compile time by a linker. In static linking, functions and variables defined in external library files are linked inside your executable. The code is actually linked against your code when compiling/linking.

Dynamic linking is done at runtime by the operating system. Static functions keep residing in the external library and are referenced by the software. Examples are *.o files in most embedded OS's and DLL files in windows OS.

195. How does the compilation/linking process work?

Answer:

The compilation of a C++ program involves three steps:

Preprocessing: The preprocessor takes a C++ source code file and deals with the #includes, #defines, and other preprocessor directives. The output of this step is a "pure" C++ file without pre-processor directives.

Compilation: The compiler takes the preprocessor's output and produces an object file from it.

Linking: The linker takes the object files produced by the compiler and produces either a library or an executable file.

Networking

196. What is IP, TCP, UDP?

Answer:

IP: IP is a network layer protocol that contains a network address and allows messages to be routed to a different network or subnet. IP does not guarantee data delivery of a complete message

TCP is a transport protocol that enables two hosts to establish a connection and exchange streams of data. TCP guarantees delivery of data and also guarantees that packets will be delivered in the same order in which they were sent. Provides Reliable Data Delivery TCP uses the unreliable IP to carry data.

UDP is a transport protocol that is used in place of TCP when a reliable delivery is not required. There is less processing of UDP packets than there is for TCP. UDP is widely used for real-time audio and video traffic where lost packets are simply ignored because there is no time to retransmit. If UDP is used and reliable delivery is required, packet sequence checking and error notification must be written into the application.

Things to consider with UDP are that UDP is a connectionless transport protocol, does not guarantee reliable data delivery. UDP messages can be lost or duplicated, or they may arrive out of order, and they can arrive faster than the receiver can process them.

197. What is a socket?

Answer:

A socket is one endpoint of a two-way communication link between two programs running on the network.

198. Compare between TCP/IP & OSI model?

Answer:

TCP/IP is the alternate model that also explains the information flow in the network. It is a simpler representation in comparison to the OSI model but contains fewer details of protocols than the OSI model.

OSI Model	TCP/IP Model
Application Layer	Application Layer
Presentation Layer	
Session Layer	
Transport Layer	Transport Layer
Network Layer	Internet Layer
Datalink Layer	Network Access Layer
Physical Layer	

199.   Is UDP better than TCP? Can you list the UDP and TCP packet formats?

Answer:

Both protocols are used for different purposes. If the user wants error-free and guarantees to deliver data, TCP is the choice. If the user wants fast transmission of data and little loss of data is not a problem, UDP is the choice.

UDP format:

Source port	Destination Port
Length	CheckSum

TCP format:

Source Port			Destination Port	
Sequence Number				
Acknowledgment Number				
Data Offset	Reserved	Code	Window	
Checksum			Urgent Pointer	
Options				Padding
Data				

200.   What is the TCP 3-way handshake?

Answer:

TCP 3-way handshake is a process that is used in a TCP/IP network to make a connection between the server and client. It is a three-step process that requires both the client and server to exchange synchronization and acknowledgment packets before the real data communication process starts.

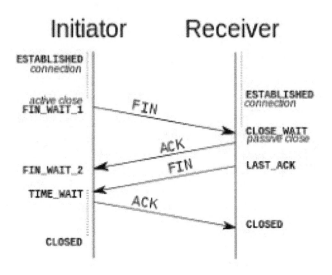

Initiator   Receiver

201. What does a socket consist of?

Answer:

The combination of an IP address and a port number is called a socket.

202. What is socket programming?

Answer:

Socket programming is a way of connecting two nodes on a network to communicate with each other. One socket(node) listens on a particular port at an IP, while another socket reaches out to the other to form a connection. The server forms the listener socket while the client reaches out to the server.

State diagram of server and client model:

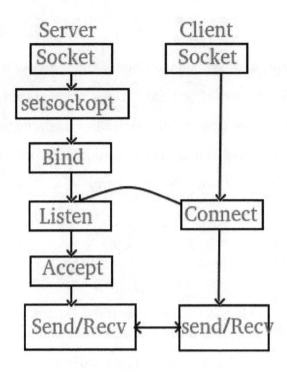

Embedded Linux

203. What is embedded Linux? Provide examples?

Answer:

Embedded Linux is a type of Linux operating system/kernel that is designed to be installed and used within embedded devices and appliances. It is a compact version of Linux that offers features and services in line with the operating and application requirement of the embedded system.

One major example of an embedded Linux is Android, developed by Google. ... Other examples of embedded Linux include Maemo, BusyBox, and Mobilinux. Debian, an open-source operating system that uses the Linux kernel, is used on the embedded Raspberry Pi device in an operating system called Raspberry.

204.   What is the difference between Linux and Embedded Linux?

Answer:

Difference Between Embedded Linux and Desktop Linux. Linux operating system is used in desktop, servers and in the embedded system also. In an embedded system it is used as a Real-Time Operating System where memory is limited, hard disk is not present, a display screen is small, etc.

205.   Which Linux OS is best for embedded development?

Answer:

One very popular non-desktop option for Linux distro for embedded systems is Yocto, also known as Openembedded. Yocto is supported by an army of open source enthusiasts, some big-name tech advocates, and lots of semiconductor and board manufacturers

206. Why Linux is used in an embedded system?

Answer:

Platform usage. The advantages of embedded Linux over proprietary embedded operating systems include multiple suppliers for software, development and support; no royalties or licensing fees; a stable kernel; the ability to read, modify and redistribute the source code.

207. What are the elements of embedded Linux?

Answer:

Every embedded Linux project begins by obtaining, customizing, and deploying these four elements: Toolchain, Bootloader, Kernel, and Root filesystem.

Toolchain - The toolchain is the first element of embedded Linux and the starting point of your project. It should be constant throughout the project, in other words, once you have chosen your toolchain it is important to stick with it. Changing compilers and development libraries in an inconsistent way during a project will lead to subtle bugs.

Bootloader - The bootloader is the second element of Embedded Linux. It is the part that starts the system up and loads the operating system kernel. When considering which bootloader to focus on, there is one that stands out: U-Boot.

In an embedded Linux system, the bootloader has two main jobs: to start the system running and to load a kernel. The first job is in somewhat subsidiary to the second in that it is only necessary to get as much of the system working as is necessary to load the kernel.

Kernel - The kernel is the third element of Embedded Linux. It is the component that is responsible for managing resources and interfacing with hardware, and so affects almost every aspect of your final software build. Usually, it is tailored to your particular hardware configuration.

The kernel has three main jobs to do: to manage resources, to interface to the hardware, and to provide an API that offers a useful level of abstraction to user space programs.

Root filesystem - The root filesystem is the fourth and final element of embedded Linux. The first objective is to create a minimal root filesystem that can give us a shell prompt. Then using that as a base we will add scripts to start other programs up, and to configure a network interface and user permissions. Knowing how to build the root filesystem from scratch is a useful skill.

208.   Can we use semaphore or mutex or spinlock in the Interrupt

context in Linux kernel?

Answer:

Semaphore or Mutex cannot be used for Interrupt context in Linux

kernel, while spinlocks can be used for locking Interrupt context

vxWorks

209.   What is vxWorks?

Answer:

vxWorks made and sold by Wind River, is a real-time operating

system. It requires a host workstation for program development.

Unlike systems such as UNIX and QNX, vxWorks development is done on a "host" machine running UNIX or Windows, cross-compiling target software to run on various target CPU architectures.

210.   What are the benefits of vxWorks and why?

Answer:

vxWorks has characteristics such as Deterministic, Multitasking, Fast Context Switching, Support for Preemptive Based Scheduling Support for Multiple Priority level, Support for Inter Task Communication, Support for Inter Task Synchronization, Low Interrupt Latency Low Memory Footprint, Scalable.

All of these make intertask communication faster and context switching latency is reduced because, all tasks reside in common address space, no swapping and paging of memory are used.

vxWorks can be scaled; unnecessary components can be easily excluded. Memory usage will be greatly reduced because of this feature.

vxWorks is extendable, new components can be added as a task

211.   What is the memory layout in vxWorks?

Answer:

The memory layout in vxWorks is known as flat physical address
space. The diagram below shows how the memory is divided into
different regions on the target board's RAM

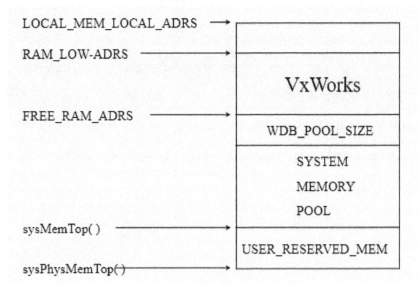

212.   What is the difference between signals and Interrupts?

Answer:

Signals will tell about some event that has occurred. But when an
Interrupt has occurred the system has to stop the current task and
has to switch to ISR

213.   What are message queues and Pipes in vxWorks?

Answer:

Message queues and pipes are a way of inter-task communication used to send and receive messages between two tasks.

Pipes are virtual I/O and unidirectional messages are sent and received in form of bytes. A message queue can be created with variable length messages that are sent by passing the address of the buffer which holds the message. message queue created with a queue length of one is called a mailbox, it can be used for synchronization.

214.   What Is the Difference B/w downloadable and Bootable Application?

Answer:

Bootable Project - A project used to configure and build vxWorks images for a particular BSP. Application code may be statically linked to such a vxWorks image, and the application's start-up code may be specified.

Downloadable Project - A project used to manage and build application modules that can be downloaded and dynamically linked with a running vxWorks image. Allows "on the fly" development.

215.   What is Tornado and its features?

Answer:

Tornado is an Integrated development environment for vxWorks 5.4. Its features include

- An integrated source-code editor.
- A project management facility.
- Integrated C and C++ compilers and make.
- The browser, Collection of visualization aids to monitor the target system.
- Crosswind, Graphically enhanced source-level debugger.
- WindSh, C-language command shell that controls the target.
- An integrated version of the vxWorks target simulator, VxSim.
- An integrated version of the WindView software logic analyzer for the target simulator.

216.   What does the target server do?

Answer:

Target server provides host-based management of target resources needed by development tools:

- Communication with debug agent on target.
- Dynamic module loading and unloading.
- The host-resident symbol table for the target.
- Allocation of memory on target for host tools.
- All Tornado tools use the Wind River Tool Exchange Protocol (WTX) to communicate with the target server. The WTX protocol is documented.

217.   What is task spawn in vxWorks?

Answer:

In vxWorks, any subroutine can be spawned as a separate task, with its own context and stack. It also allows this spawned task to be suspended, resumed, deleted, delayed and moved in priority

218.   What are message queues and pipes?

Answer:

Message queues and pipes are a way of inter-task communication used to send and receive messages between two tasks.

Pipes are virtual and unidirectional messages are sent and received in form of bytes. A message queue can be created with variable length messages that are sent by passing address of the buffer which holds the message . message queue created with queue length of one is called as mailbox , it can be used for synchronization.

- User reserved memory
- System memory pool
- WDB_POOL_SIZE
- vxWorks + application
- Interrupt vector
- table,bootline, exception message

219.   How is vxWorks different from UNIX or Linux OS?

Answer:

vxWorks runs in one mode. No protected vs. user mode switching is done. Running in supervisor mode on most processors, and not using traps for system calls. UNIX provides resource reclamation; by default, vxWorks does not. vxWorks does not have full "process"; it only has tasks, or "threads".

220. What are the differences between traditional UNIX and vxWorks?

Answer:

vxWorks does have a lot of UNIX "compatible" routines in the user libraries. So, porting a UNIX application is not that hard. But there are enough differences to make such a port take longer than normally expected.

vxWorks runs in one mode. No protected vs. user mode switching is done. Running in supervisor mode on most processors, and not using traps for system calls, vxWorks can achieve minimal overhead on a given piece of hardware than UNIX. Programming on vxWorks can be trickier than UNIX for the same reason.

UNIX provides resource reclamation; by default, vxWorks does not. [editorial: using deleteHooks or whatever, you could implement this on your own.] Instead programmers write what they need as needed. As a result, the context switch time in vxWorks is on the order of a few

micro-seconds (since there is a lot smaller context to save and restore). vxWorks does not have full "process"; it only has tasks, or "threads", or lightweight processes as some people like to call them.

Like any other multi-threaded environment (or MP environments), care should be taken when writing multi-tasking code. Each routine should be written carefully to be re-entrant (if it is going to be called from multiple contexts), semaphores are used a lot for this. And static variables are frowned upon. Sometimes, when porting a UNIX application, you may need to add "task variables" for this reason (as done for rpcLib in vxWorks).

vxWorks: minimal Interrupt latency (e.g. spl's are quasi-implemented as semaphores). Traditional UNIX: high Interrupt latency (e.g. spl's are implemented as Interrupt lock and unlock calls).

vxWorks: priority Interrupt-driven preemption, optional round-robin time-slicing. Traditional UNIX: prioritized round-robin preemptive time-slicing. Since vxWorks is just a glorified "program" it can be changed and customized pretty easily. Task scheduling can be customized as desired, for example.

vxWorks networking code, however, is very UNIX compatible [editorial: it is essentially "ported" version of BSD UNIX TCP/IP code. It is relatively easy to port socket based code to vxWorks.

vxWorks most definitely is not a "real-time UNIX", or a variant of UNIX as often misunderstood by some people. The confusion perhaps is due to the fact that UNIX hosts are used most widely to develop applications for vxWorks (and vxWorks itself).

There are a lot more differences! In short, UNIX is a nice system to run emacs on. vxWorks is much better at playing pin-ball game machines.

Having said all this, I should also note that there are Realtime capable UNIX systems out there. Most of these systems do not come close to the capabilities and performance of vxWorks in real-time processing.

An exception to this might be QNX, which is a very well designed Realtime POSIX operating system.

221. What kind of products has been developed using vxWorks?

Answer:

- Flight simulators
- Radio and optical telescopes
- Automotive ABS & real-time suspension
- Navigation systems
- Deep sea instrumentation
- PBXs
- Traffic control systems
- Modems
- Sonar systems
- Comm/weather satellite test equipment
- PostScript laser printers
- robotics

- NFS protocol accelerator product
- mass storage tape robot systems

222. How does vxWorks system calls work?

Answer:

vxWorks does not have the concept of "system call". Unlike Operating Systems such as pSOS, VRTX, Unix, and many others, vxWorks calls are C function subroutines just like any other function call you may implement yourself. There is really no distinction between a "system call" and a generic C subroutine call.

223. Why can't I call printf() inside Interrupt service routines?

Answer: In general, within an Interrupt service routine, you cannot call any routines that can potentially block waiting for resources. Nor would you really want to (think about it). The printf() routine can block on a semaphore trying to get access to the output device until it becomes available. A workaround is to call logMsg(). The logMsg() routine works by queueing your message content via a message queue. It is sent to logTask, which prints it out at a task level when logTask gets to run as deemed proper by the scheduler.

224. Is there a better malloc/free replacement that does not fragment as badly?

Answer:

There is a port of malloc library that consists of two algorithms that are different than original vxWorks memLib. VxHacks archive contains this port which has BSD and Doug Lea's malloc libraries.

225. Is there a better malloc/free replacement that does not fragment as badly?

Answer:

There is a port of malloc library that consists of two algorithms that are different than original vxWorks memLib. VxHacks archive contains this port which has BSD and Doug Lea's malloc libraries.

226. What is saving and restoring floating point registers per context switch and in an ISR?

Answer:

To indicate that your task is using floating point registers which should be saved and restored per context switch, you should not forget to set VX_FP_TASK option in your task. Your ISR (Interrupt Service Routines) should call fppSave() and fppRestore() if it uses

180

floating point registers. Depending on your compiler, it might be necessary to encapsulate your ISR in another dummy routine. For example, a certain version of m68040 GNU compilers generate references to floating point registers even before your C code is generated. To avoid problems with these cases, you can create a C function that calls fppSave() and then calls your real ISR routine, and then calls fppRestore(), as a workaround.

227. What are vxWorks "watchdog" related common errors?

Answer:

The watchdog timer (wdLib) is a generic timer and not necessarily closely related to hardware watchdog facility available in many systems. It can certainly be used in association with a hardware watchdog resetting mechanism, but the name is a little bit of a misnomer.

A common error in using watchdog timer has to do with calling routines that can block. Since the watchdog timer routine itself runs at Interrupt level, you should not call any routines that can block. A frequent mistake is to call printf() inside a watchdog timer handler routine. You can use logMsg() instead.

228.   What are the common parameters to tune for better network performance on vxWorks?

Answer:

Using setsockopt() call, you can change the socket level buffer sizes of TCP sockets. This can affect the sizes of buffer windows TCP protocol uses which can have a different performance impact. The options are SO_SNDBUF and SO_RCVBUF.

You can also tune global variables: tcp_sendspace, tcp_recvspace, udp_sendspace, and udp_recvspace. Read original BSD TCP/IP code before attempting to change these globals.

To get around some latency related problems, you may turn on TCP_NODELAY option on TCP sockets which disables Nagle's algorithm.

Additionally, there are various mbuf pool parameters in various configurable source files in your BSP.

229.   Can I get multiple target shell sessions via telnet?

Answer:

vxWorks target shell is non-reentrant and the only single instance is allowed to run at a time. The telnet daemon in vxWorks only allows a single login session at a time. This is due to the way a single console descriptor is shared globally, among other things.

An alternative is to use winsh from Tornado which will allow multiple target shell-like sessions. However, winsh does not have all the facilities one might expect and it is not entirely compatible with the original target shell. Some of the commands available in target shell are not available in winsh and vice versa.

Internet of Things (IoT)

230.   What is IoT and how does it work?

Answer:

IoT stands for the Internet of things refers to the interconnection of the network of various devices that can recognize, collect, and transfer data over the internet without human involvement.

It is a group of objects which we use in day to day life linked to a network. The objects embedded with the micro-controller, software, and sensors that enable these objects to recognize, collect, and communicate with one another and users, playing a vital role on the Internet.

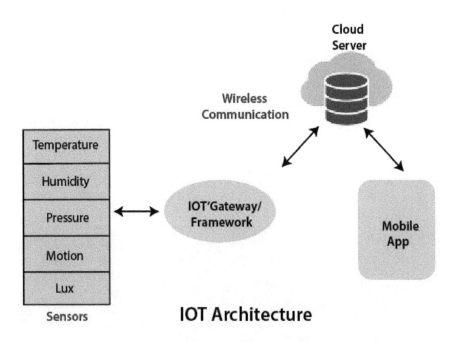

IOT Architecture

The IoT Model makes the web more insistent by easy access and communication with various devices. For example, surveillance cameras, home appliances sensors, and many more. The Internet of things executed for the advancement of application that uses the data generated by the objects to provide services.

231.   Describe the different components of IoT?

Answer:

An IoT device typically comprises four major components.

Sensors – Much of IoT involves environment adaptability and the major factor contributing to it is the sensors in the IoT devices. Sensors are devices that enable IoT devices to gather data from their surroundings. Effectively, they may be perceived as instruments that sense the environment and perform multiple tasks. Sensors make the IoT devices capable of real-world integration. It can be of varied types. From a simple GPS in your phones to the live video feature on a social media platform.

Connectivity- With the advent of cloud computing, devices can be launched on a cloud platform, and in the due course, devices can interact freely with each other at a cheaper and more transparent scale. For IoT devices, cloud computing facilitates freedom from exclusive network providers. Instead, small network connection mediums like mobile satellite networks, WAN, Bluetooth, etc. are used.

Data Processing – As soon as the environmental stimuli are gathered by the sensors and transmuted to the cloud, it is the job of the data processors to process the information collected and perform the required tasks. From adjusting the temperatures of the AC to facial recognition on mobile phones or biometric devices, data processing software is largely responsible for enhancing the automation in IoT devices.

User Interface – The IoT introduced a new paradigm among the available devices for active interaction and engagement. This has transformed the user interface widely. Instead of one-way communication mechanisms of traditional devices, IoT enables cascading effects on end-user commands. This is precisely why IoT devices are all the more communicative and active.

232.   What is the use of BLE in IoT?

Answer:

Unlike classic Bluetooth, BLE remains in sleep mode constantly except for when a connection is initiated. It is used in applications that do not need to exchange large amounts of data and can, therefore, run on battery power for years at a cheaper cost, therefore it is used as one of the means of exchanging data between the devices.

233. What are the benefits and challenges of IoT?

Answer:

Benefits are :

Automation and control -The Internet of things permit you to automate and control the tasks which are performed in day to day life.

Better efficiency - Machine to Machine communication provides better results with more transparency. Moreover, people can free to do other jobs.

Challenges are :

Privacy and security - Managing privacy settings on the Internet is essential. Many of our day to day life machines, appliances, and services become connected to the Internet with certain information available on the Internet which makes it harder to keep confidential information from the data breached and spammers.

Complexity - Internet of things is such an extensive, distinct network, A single error in software or hardware may cause significant consequences.

234. Name some of the various sectors where IoT played a major role?

Answer:

IoT is covering almost all sectors. Some important major sectors are as follows:

- Manufacturing
- logistics(GPS tracking)
- Real Estate and Housing(smart homes)
- Health care(Telemedicine)
- Agriculture

235. What are the security concerns related to IoT?

Answer:

Data security and privacy are major concerns related to IoT. These devices are vulnerable to hacking and cloud endpoints could be used by hackers to attack servers. Software developers and device designers have to ensure adequate security and privacy measures.

236. Explain the IoT protocol stack?

Answer:

IoT has 4 protocol layers:

- Sensing and information: Includes various smart sensor devices based on GPS, RFID, Wi-Fi, etc.

- Network connectivity: Layer is based on a wired and wireless network such as WLAN, WMAN, Ethernet, optical fiber, and more.
- Information processing layer
- Application layer

237.   What is the top 5 Machine to Machine (M2M) applications?

Answer:

Some of the examples are as follows:

- Asset tracking and monitoring in some form or some other (stolen automobiles, fleet, construction system, and many others seems to be the biggest.
- Insurance telematics is huge as it gives insurance groups the possibility to cut the threat and force higher/extra appealing pricing.
- Utilities/automatic meter reading/clever grids – plenty of regulation and funding into this in the intervening time. There plenty of countrywide solutions because the requirements and business cases are driven in very numerous ways.
- Automotive is also very big and is driven by consumer's demand.
- mHealth is also present in a small scale.

238. What Is The difference between IoT and Machine to Machine (m2m)?

Answer:

The difference between the two of them can be summarized as below

IoT	M2M
Digital connectivity among various devices to communicate	Devices connected to the formwork cycle using various machines and devices
Random work, work instructions are given among devices	The action triggered events among devices
Interchange of data is huge as it involves devices, machines, people, things, etc	Cloud computing helps in interacting/data exchange
Sensor integrated devices to enable IoT connectivity	Wired, wireless, cellular, etc
Two-way communication offers an option to all the devices	Mostly one way, based on triggered actions
Solution managing all the connections offer unlimited integration	Requires particular communication rules, resulting in minimal integration
Need internet for most of the cases	No need to rely on the internet

239.   What is Industrial Internet of Things (IIoT)?

Answer:

The Industrial Internet of Things (IIoT) is the use of Internet of Things (IoT) technologies in manufacturing.

While the Internet of Things (IoT) refers to the consumer-oriented gadgets which perform tasks that provide consumer utilities like smartphones, thermostats, etc., business IoT or IIoT are large scale structures or systems that are usually used at the industrial levels. For instance, fire alarms, etc. Since the major difference lies in the scale of impact, a failure in IIoT is likely to affect a wider range of the population.

Also known as the Industrial Internet, IIoT incorporates machine learning and big data technology, harnessing the sensor data, machine-to-machine (M2M) communication, and automation technologies that have existed in industrial settings for years. The driving philosophy behind the IIoT is that smart machines are better than humans at accurately, consistently capturing and communicating data. This data can enable companies to pick up on inefficiencies and problems sooner, saving time and money and supporting business intelligence efforts. In manufacturing specifically, IIoT holds great potential for quality control, sustainable and green practices, supply chain traceability, and overall supply chain efficiency.

240. What are the main challenges of implementing IoT?

Answer:

The first and foremost issue with implementing Internet of Things(IoT) is the Security aspect. As the data is exchanged over the internet it is very easy for cybercriminals to come up with a system that can actually break into the network and steal valuable information. Consider the above scenario happening in the healthcare industry where the patient records are exposed to the public.

As the devices are connected to a single network, it is easy for cybercriminals to inject a virus which can totally damage the entire hardware which results in a huge loss. This can also happen if we have not focused much on the security aspects.

241. What are the industrial applications for wireless sensor networks Internet of Things (IoT)?

Answer:

You can easily and cheaply buy sensors that can measure a variety of variables that would be interesting in industrial applications, for example (and this is for sure not a complete list): light or sound intensity; voltage; current; pressure; temperature; rotational position; XYZ orientation; compass direction; acceleration; location; fluid flow rate and so on.

These sensors can be interrogated by the microcontroller, and data stored to memory card or communicated in real-time to other systems via Bluetooth, Zigbee, Wi-Fi, Ethernet, serial, USB, infrared and so on.

The inexpensive nature of these microcontrollers (for example Google for ESP8266 to see a WIFI-enabled microcontroller) means that you could deploy a large number of these in an industrial setting (even in hazardous environments) and gather data without large capital investment and without the worry of "what if it gets destroyed"?

There must be so many industrial applications of this technology that it's impossible to enumerate the possibilities. The limiting factor is really only "how can we process all of this data"?

242. What is the difference between IoT devices and embedded devices?

Answer:

Internet of things is a type of embedded system that connects to the internet. Embedded systems tend to be small software programs that implement a few functions. Internet of Things may be updated constantly according to the environment and learn by itself.

243. What are the most used sensors types in IoT?

Answer:

Some of the most commonly used sensors are:

- Temperature sensors
- Proximity sensor
- Pressure sensor
- Gas sensor
- Smoke sensor
- IR sensors
- Motion detection sensors

244. Can you list out some of water sensors?

Answer:

- Total organic carbon sensor
- Turbidity sensor
- Conductivity sensor
- pH sensor

245. What is data collection in IoT?

Answer:

This software system manages sensing, measurements, light-weight information filtering, light-weight information security, and aggregation of knowledge. It uses bound protocols to assist sensors in connecting with the period, machine-to-machine networks.

Then it collects information from multiple devices and distributes it in accordance with settings. It additionally works in reverse by distributing information over devices.

246. What is IoT cloud?

Answer:

The Salesforce IoT Cloud may be a platform for storing and process IoT information. It makes use of the Thunder engine for a climbable, duration match process. It's an assortment of application development elements, referred to as Lightning, powers its applications.

It gathers information from devices, websites, applications, customers, and partners to trigger movements for period responses.

247. What role does network play in the IoT?

Answer:

Network plays a necessary position in the word of the Internet of Things; it is a driving issue for bringing all the distinct systems together which work hand in hand and exhibit us a better future or betterment in every process. It gives an intelligent, manageable, and secure infrastructure for better execution.

248. What is the difference between IoT devices and embedded devices?

Answer:

Internet of things is a type of embedded system that connects to the Internet. Embedded systems tend to be small software programs that implement a few functions. Internet of Things may be updated constantly according to the environment and learn by itself.

249. What is sharding?

Answer:

Sharding is the process of Splitting data into multiple collections and store the data multiple machines.

250. What is the difference b/w a wireless sensor network (WSN) and the IoT network?

Answer:

WSN: Wi-Fi sensor community is the foundation of IoT packages. WSN is a network of wireless sensors, fashioned to look at, to take a look at, or to monitor bodily parameters of desired utility. e.g. wireless sensors deployed in agricultural land, screen temp-humidity, or maybe soil moisture, who gathers statistics and ideal statistics analysis procedure consequences approximately crop yields-high quality or amount.

IoT: IoT is a community of bodily objects managed and monitored over the Internet. Now just as win, in its application, you will stumble upon the monitoring of physical parameters. But preferred results are a little different. IoT is about M2M, it's far greater than bringing smartness into daily gadgets. e.g. device hooked in your thermostat monitors surrounding temperature and adjusts it to maximum favored.

251.   Why is Zigbee protocol so important for the Internet of Things implementation?

Answer:

The Zigbee Protocol is very important because it is known for its low power consumption, it maintained IEEE 802.15.4 (2003) standards while utilization.

252. Explain Bluetooth Low Energy (BLE) Protocol for Internet of Things (IoT)?

Answer:

Nokia originally introduced this protocol as Wibree in 2006. Also known as Blue tooth Smart this protocol provides the same range coverage with much-reduced power consumption as the original Blue tooth. It has similar bandwidth with narrow spacing as used by ZigBee. Low power latency and lower complexity make BLE more suitable to incorporate into low-cost microcontrollers.

Low power latency and lower complexity make BLE more suitable to incorporate into low-cost microcontrollers. As far as the application is concerned BLE is in the health care sector. As wearable health monitors are becoming prevalent the sensors of these devices can easily communicate with a smartphone or any medical instrument regularly using BLE protocol.

253. What are the most commonly used protocols in IoT?

Answer:

Some of the protocols used are :

- MQTT protocol
- XMPP
- AMQP

- Data Distribution Service (DDS)
- Simple Text Oriented Messaging Protocol(STOMP)
- Very Simple Control Protocol (VSCP)
- Zigbee
- Wi-Fi

254.   What is meant by a smart city in the context of IoT?

Answer:

As with IoT and other popular technology terms, there is no established consensus definition or set of criteria for characterizing what a smart city is. Specific characterizations vary widely, but in commonplace they involve the use of IoT and b technologies to improve energy, transportation, governance, and other municipal services for specified goals such as sustainability or accelerated quality of life.

The related technologies include:

- Social media (such as Face book and Twitter)
- Mobile computing (such as smartphones and wearable devices)
- Data Analytics (Big Data – the processing and use of very massive data sets; and open facts? databases that are publicly accessible).

- Cloud computing (the delivery of computing services from a remote location, analogous to the way utilities such as electrical energy are provided).
- Together, these are sometimes known as SMAC.

255. What sensor and actuator are used to control any home appliances from any IoT devices in wired mode?

Answer:

A relay is used to control any home appliances from any IoT or Embedded devices. A relay is nothing but an electrically operated switch.

256. What are suitable databases for Iot?

Answer:

Below are the databases the are widely used in an IoT environment:

- influxDB,
- Mongodb,
- RethinkDB,
- Sqlite
- Apache Cassandra

257. What are the enabling factors of IoT?

Answer:

The main enabling factors for the IoT are as follows:

- New, mature sensors with more capabilities and high performance at a low cost.
- New networks and wireless connectivity (such as PAN and LAN) interconnecting the sensors and devices to optimize the bandwidth, power consumption, latency, and range.
- New, powerful, and cheap processors and microprocessors coming from the mobile devices' world.
- Real-time operating systems, leading to a more sophisticated and powerful integrated development platform at the maker's disposal.
- Virtualization technology, which divides naturally into the data center, big data, and the cloud.
- The diffusion of mobile devices.

258. What is an IoT platform?

Answer:

An IoT platform provides users with one or more of these key elements — visualization tools, data security features, a workflow engine, and a custom user interface to utilize the information collected from devices and other data sources in the field. Cloud platforms are based in the cloud and can be accessed from anywhere.

259. What is edge computing?

Answer:

Edge computing is a method that enables devices to process data at or near where it is collected instead of sending it to a data center or to the cloud. Edge computing is used to achieve local optimized control, operate in spite of intermittent connectivity, or immediately filter data, sending only what is necessary to the cloud.

260. What is Condition-based maintenance?

Answer:

Condition-based maintenance or CBM is a method of proactive maintenance that enables owners to respond to conditions only when a need arises. Conditions of machine components are monitored using IoT (sensors, a network connection, and gateways).

261. What is predictive maintenance?

Answer:

Predictive maintenance refers to a method of maintenance created using IoT that relies on data from a combination of sources including machine components and other indicators that inform an owner/operator of the items requiring attention before any service Interruption occurs. Predictive maintenance often requires a large supply of historical data in order to function appropriately.

262.   What impact will IoT have on the Manufacturing sector?

Answer:

The integration of IoT technologies into manufacturing and supply chain logistics is predicted to have a transformative effect on the sector. The biggest impact may be realized in the optimization of operations, making manufacturing processes more efficient. Efficiencies can be achieved by connecting components of factories to optimize production, but also by connecting components of inventory and shipping for supply chain optimization.

Another application is predictive maintenance, which uses sensors to monitor machinery and factory infrastructure for damage. Resulting data can enable maintenance crews to replace parts before potentially dangerous and/or costly malfunctions occur.

263. What is IoT ThingWorx?

Answer:

ThingWorx is a platform for sustainable development and implementation of active connected devices. It is a combination of IoT enhancement tool which supports analysis, production, connectivity, and other aspects of IoT Enhancement.

264. Explain IoT GE Predix?

Answer:

In IoT GE Predix, GE stands for "General Electronic", In Other Words, we can say that IoT GE Predix. It is a Software Platform for the collection and examination of data; generated as sensors attached from the various Instruments(Electrical or Mechanical) used in the industries such as Healthcare, Aviation, Energy, and transportation.

IoT GE Predix produces a cloud-based PaaS (Platform as a service). It allows Industrial-scale analytics for Performance management and operational development which provides better and faster decision making and an excellent way to interconnect data, machine, and people. Every Layer of the platform has high-security protection. Many different services (Data Privacy, Authentication, User management, Authorization) help to minimize the risk associated with programs.

265. What is Big Data and How it is related to IoT?

Answer:

Big data relates to a massive amount of data that can be unstructured, semi-structured, and structured. It can extract data for information used in advanced analytics applications and machine learning projects.

Big data generally described by 3vs concept:

- Volume - Previously, collecting data would have been a tough task- but the innovation of new technologies has eased the burden. Nowadays, many organizations collect data from various sources, including social media platforms, business transactions via sensors or machine to machine data.

- Velocity - Velocity refers to the speed with which data generated. Consider an example of social media insights, 500 Million tweets are posted on Twitter every day, 900 Million photos uploaded on Facebook daily. Big data helps the company to collect the data from the flow of data, and at the same time, frame processes the data so that it doesn't slow down the process.

- Variety - Variety in Big Date Includes Structured, Semi-structured, and unstructured data that has the probability of getting generated either by machines or humans. For example, ECG reading, Handwritten text, tweets, Emails, etc. Variety in Big Data can also be defined as the ability to arrange incoming data from various categories.

Azure IoT

266. What is Azure IoT?

Answer:

The Azure Internet of Things (IoT) is a collection of Microsoft-managed cloud services that connect, monitor and control billions of IoT assets. In simpler terms, an IoT solution is made up of one or more IoT devices that communicate with one or more back-end services hosted in the cloud.

267. What is Windows 10 IoT Core?

Answer:

Windows 10 IoT Core is a full-fledged operating system based on Windows 10 specifically designed to operate on embedded devices. This will empower you to build a single universal app experience.

268. What is Azure RTOS?

Answer:

Azure RTOS is an embedded development suite including a small but powerful operating system that provides reliable, ultra-fast performance for resource-constrained devices. It's easy-to-use and market-proven, having been deployed on more than 6.2 billion devices worldwide. Azure RTOS supports the most popular 32-bit microcontrollers and embedded development tools, so you can make the most of your team's existing skills.

269.   What is Azure IoT Edge?

Answer:

Azure IoT Edge moves cloud analytics and custom business logic to devices so that your organization can focus on business insights instead of data management. Scale-out your IoT solution by packaging your business logic into standard containers, then you can deploy those containers to any of your devices and monitor it all from the cloud.

Analytics drives business value in IoT solutions, but not all analytics needs to be in the cloud. If you want to respond to emergencies as quickly as possible, you can run anomaly detection workloads at the edge. If you want to reduce bandwidth costs and avoid transferring terabytes of raw data, you can clean and aggregate the data locally then only send the insights to the cloud for analysis.

Azure IoT Edge is made up of three components:

- IoT Edge modules are containers that run Azure services, third-party services, or your own code. Modules are deployed to IoT Edge devices and execute locally on those devices.
- The IoT Edge runtime runs on each IoT Edge device and manages the modules deployed to each device.
- A cloud-based interface enables you to remotely monitor and manage IoT Edge devices.

270. What is Azure IoT Hub?

Answer:

IoT Hub is a managed service, hosted in the cloud, that acts as a central message hub for bi-directional communication between your IoT application and the devices it manages. You can use Azure IoT Hub to build IoT solutions with reliable and secure communications between millions of IoT devices and a cloud-hosted solution backend. You can connect virtually any device to IoT Hub.

IoT Hub supports communications both from the device to the cloud and from the cloud to the device. IoT Hub supports multiple messaging patterns such as device-to-cloud telemetry, file upload from devices, and request-reply methods to control your devices from the cloud. IoT Hub monitoring helps you maintain the health of your solution by tracking events such as device creation, device failures, and device connections.

IoT Hub's capabilities help you build scalable, full-featured IoT solutions such as managing industrial equipment used in manufacturing, tracking valuable assets in healthcare, and monitoring office building usage

225. What are Azure Digital Twins?

Answer:

Azure Digital Twins is an IoT platform that enables the creation of comprehensive digital models of entire environments. These environments could be buildings, factories, farms, energy networks, railways, stadiums, and more—even entire cities. These digital models can be used to gain insights that drive better products, optimized operations, reduced costs, and breakthrough customer experiences.

Customer leverage domain expertise on top of Azure Digital Twins to build customized, connected solutions that:

- Model any environment, and bring digital twins to life in a scalable and secure manner
- Connect assets such as IoT devices and existing business systems

- Use a robust event system to build dynamic business logic and data processing
- Integrate with Azure data, analytics, and AI services to help you track the past and then predict the future

271. What are the azure technologies/services available for creating IoT solutions?

Answer:

Azure IoT technologies and services provide you with options to create a wide variety of IoT solutions that enable digital transformation for your organization. For example, you can:

Use Azure IoT Central, a managed IoT application platform, to build and deploy a secure, enterprise-grade IoT solution. IoT Central features a collection of industry-specific application templates, such as retail and healthcare, to accelerate your solution development process.

Extend the open-source codebase for an Azure IoT solution accelerator to implement a common IoT scenario such as remote monitoring or predictive maintenance.

Use Azure IoT platform services such as Azure IoT Hub and the Azure IoT device SDKs to build a custom IoT solution from scratch.

Azure IoT technologies, services, and solutions

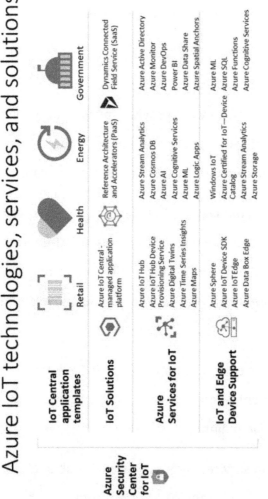

	Retail	Health	Energy	Government
IoT Central application templates				
IoT Solutions	Azure IoT Central - managed application platform		Reference Architecture and Accelerators (PaaS)	Dynamics Connected Field Service (SaaS)
Azure Services for IoT	Azure IoT Hub Azure IoT Hub Device Provisioning Service Azure Digital Twins Azure Time Series Insights Azure Maps		Azure Stream Analytics Azure Cosmos DB Azure AI Azure Cognitive Services Azure ML Azure Logic Apps	Azure Active Directory Azure Monitor Azure DevOps Power BI Azure Data Share Azure Spatial Anchors Azure ML Azure SQL Azure Functions Azure Cognitive Services
IoT and Edge Device Support	Azure Sphere Azure IoT Device SDK Azure IoT Edge Azure Data Box Edge		Windows IoT Azure Certified for IoT—Device Catalog Azure Stream Analytics Azure Storage	

Azure Security Center for IoT

AWS IoT

272. How does AWS IoT?

Answer:

AWS IoT provides secure, bi-directional communication between Internet-connected devices such as sensors, actuators, embedded micro-controllers, or smart appliances, and the AWS Cloud. This enables you to collect telemetry data from multiple devices and store and analyze the data. You can also create applications that enable your users to control these devices from their phones or tablets.

273. What are AWS IoT services?

Answer:

It provides the following services:

- Device Services to connect devices and operate them at the edge
  - FreeRTOS – Real-time operating system for microcontrollers
  - Greengrass - Local compute, messaging, data management, sync, and ML inference capabilities to edge devices
- Connectivity and Control Services
  - Core – Easily and securely connect devices to the cloud. Reliably scale to billions of devices and trillions of messages.

- o Device Defender – Security management for IoT devices
- o Device Management - Register, organize, monitor, and remotely manage connected devices at scale
- Analytics Services
  - o Analytics - Analytics for IoT devices
  - o SiteWise - easily collects, organizes and analyzes data from industrial equipment at scale
  - o Events – easily detect and respond to events from IoT sensors and applications
  - o Things Graph - Visually develop IoT applications

274. What type of IoT Solution Resources are available in AWS IoT?

Answer:

Below are some of the popular solution resources :

- Connected vehicle
- IoT for Edge
- Industrial IoT
- IoT for Connected home
- Extract, Transform, Load (ETL) with Greengrass

275. What is FreeRTOS?

Answer:

FreeRTOS is an open-source, real-time operating system for microcontrollers that makes small, low-power edge devices easy to program, deploy, secure, connect, and manage. Distributed freely under the MIT open source license, FreeRTOS includes a kernel and a growing set of software libraries suitable for use across industry sectors and applications.

276.   What is AWS IoT Core?

Answer:

AWS IoT Core is a managed cloud platform that lets connected devices easily and securely interact with cloud applications and other devices. AWS IoT Core can support billions of devices and trillions of messages and can process and route those messages to AWS endpoints and to other devices reliably and securely. With AWS IoT Core, your applications can keep track of and communicate with all your devices, all the time, even when they aren't connected.

Conclusion

Congratulations! You are ready to face job interviews now. In the next interview when you get a question you know what to do.

Thank you!

I hope you have enjoyed this book and found it useful. I hope you will recommend it to your friends or consider writing a review on Amazon.

Just email a screenshot of your "Verified purchase" review to OutcomesFoundry@gmail.com to get a free copy of our professionally done resume template.

Thank you for reading and wish you all the Best!

Akram

About the Author

Akram Mohammad is a passionate product leader with a 20-year track record of building and launching embedded software and the Internet of things products.

Akram Mohammad has worked for Dell, General Electric, Intel, Qualcomm, and Nokia as a product Management and Engineering professional. Where he has interviewed and hired hundreds of candidates.

In this book, he will be sharing tips and advice on how to prepare, execute, and follow-up to get the job you want in the Embedded software and Internet of things space.

Akram holds a master's in computer science from the University of Louisiana and an MBA from UCLA Anderson school of management. He lives in Austin, Texas